"Part memoir and part detective story, Rhonda Noonan's *Fifth and Final Name* is a fascinating coming-of-age story that should be hailed by all adopted Americans. Actually, Noonan's final name is not Churchill—it's Persistence—and that's her first name, too. The book brilliantly personifies her grandfather's famous quotation: 'Never, never, never give up!' And there is an honest, earnest, informal charm in her tone that will make all readers root for her through her astonishing journey from curiosity through frustration to richly deserved self-knowledge."

—Dr. Elliot Engel, English Professor,
North Carolina State University

"Through thirty years of battling the court system and overcoming many obstacles on the way to finding her birth family, Rhonda takes us inside the world of closed-record adoptions and blows it wide open! *The Fifth and Final Name* is a beautifully written memoir and a powerful treatise on adoptee rights—a triumph."

—Spencer Lord, author of *The Brain Mechanic*
and Co-Founder of Ekta Transglobal Foundation

"Adopted people everywhere will relate to Rhonda's deep passion and inner desire to search for the deeply buried mystery of her origins. Her heart and strength shine through as she invites the reader to walk right along beside her, through every page-turning discovery. Hers is a life-long journey filled with intrigue and hope."

—Samantha Franklin, Oklahoma Representative,
American Adoption Congress

# The Fifth and Final Name

# The Fifth and Final Name

*Memoir of an*
*American Churchill*

RHONDA NOONAN

Chumbolly
Press

Copyright © 2013 by Rhonda Noonan

Published by Chumbolly Press
223 N. Sunset Ave.
Sand Springs, Oklahoma 74063

Manufactured in the United States of America

ISBN: 978-0-9886597-1-1
ISBN: 978-0-9886597-0-4

0 9 8 7 6 5 4 3 2 1


Cover and interior design by Sheila Hart Design, Inc.

Photo Credits
Pages 72, 73 (top and bottom), 74, 75 (top and bottom), 76 (top and bottom),
77, and 220 from the author's private collection.
Page 214 (top) courtesy of Zippy Thompson; (bottom) courtesy of Getty Images.
Page 215, 216, 217, 218 and 221 courtesy of Getty Images.
Page 219, courtesy of *Tulsa World*.


To view the documents referred to in this book,
please go to www.thefifthandfinalname.com

*For my Mom, Jean Noonan*

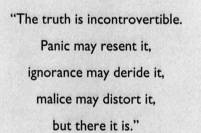

"The truth is incontrovertible.

Panic may resent it,

ignorance may deride it,

malice may distort it,

but there it is."

———

*Winston Churchill*

# ACKNOWLEDGMENTS

This beautifully crafted book is, in large part, due to the very excellent work of Laura Ross and Sheila Hart. I appreciate you both so much!

This journey was one of faith, hope, and a masterfully orchestrated patchwork of synchronicities. While I am incredibly blessed with many friends who have encouraged and cheered for me over the years, there are a few who have gone above and beyond to help me find the truth. Without this extraordinary group of people I might have collapsed into hopelessness many years ago. Lillie Werther was my friend and inspiration, cheerleader and confidante. Many a day, full of frustration and doubt, I headed down the highway to Cleveland where she welcomed and assured me that all would be well. Thanks to Monica Cervanyk, whose skills and kindness have kept the lines of communication with Lillie open to this day. Much love to Linda Colvard, search angel extraordinaire, who raises the bar for all of us trying to live a life of compassion and kindness. Appreciation all-around to Steve Turnbo, Bill Doenges, Spencer Lord, Alison Larkin, Dhiana Clarice, Chris Taylor, Kellie Watts, and the late Michael Sands. An enormous debt of gratitude to the late Polly Hunt, whose courage in speaking the truth was the defining moment in this saga. Starwalter, Harriet, Shannon, and O'Dell…I love you guys. I could not have done this without your support and kindness. Thanks and love, to Mom for never asking, "why do you need to find them?" but rather offering to "help any way I can." To my Gran and Pa…I know you are watching these proceedings. Know that I love you SO much. And, finally, a tip of the hat to my Grandfather Winston, whose life and legacy define tenacity, audacity, and possibility.

Boundless gratitude,
Rhonda

"When you have an

important point to make,

don't try to be subtle or

clever. Use a pile driver.

Hit the point once.

Then come back and hit it again.

Then hit it a third time—

a tremendous whack."

*Winston Churchill*

# "The slow and laborious task of years"

This is the story of how I discovered my fifth and final name. I was born Rene Irene Gafford, but was referred to as "Baby Girl Kim" by the Department of Human Services; after which I was renamed Rhonda Noonan. I was informed, later still, that I was Rhonda Schultz, then Rhonda Mosier. Finally, after locating and interviewing the assistant to the Director of the Oklahoma Department of Human Services (who personally handled my adoption), I discovered that my genetic father was Randolph Churchill—the son of Sir Winston Churchill.

I was adopted in a state with closed adoption records. It took me thirty years of searching—decades of painstakingly chiseling my way through institutional obfuscation and stonewalling; of endless judges, attorneys, and detectives; of hundreds of filings, mountains of paperwork, and thousands of dollars in expenses; of tackling city after city, person after person, town after town, tracking down lead after lead—to unearth my true history.

Nearly everyone involved in deciding what would happen to me had a choice to make: my birthmother made the choice to give me away; the state made a choice to take custody of me and give me away again; my adoptive parents made a choice to bring me into their home and raise me.

My birthmother's decision converted me into a sort of

commodity of the state. Every party involved in this *commoditization of me* was consciously fulfilling his or her desires. That's what commoditization is, after all.

My birthmother desired freedom from the consequences of her actions: the wholesale abdication of all responsibility for my existence. Her desires were met. The state desired to participate in the adoption services market. Its desires were met. My adoptive parents desired a child to bring up as part of their family. Their desires were met. Everyone involved in deciding my fate made conscious choices to satisfy their own desires, then had their desires met.

Everyone, that is, but me. No one ever asked what *I* wanted. My desires—past, present, and future—would be rabidly disregarded.

Fair enough; I was too young to articulate my own wishes, but surely someone would anticipate them and make some accommodation for them at a later date. Surely someone would weigh my desires on the scale with everyone else's. Surely I, too, would be able to make some choices about my life and my future—right?

Wrong.

Not only did the institutions and individuals responsible for sealing my fate ignore my desires, they actually set up a gigantic and infinitely complex machine designed to thwart all my future attempts to satisfy them, or to exercise my choices. Everyone else in the *commoditization of me* had their desires clearly articulated—and met. Yet my desires were expunged from the entire equation.

Why?

Well, here's the insidious part: my desires *had* to be expunged from the equation for it to effectively meet the desires of the people who commoditized me. In order for the state to be able to secure my transfer into their hands, they needed to promise the woman who conceived me that they would shield her from the laws of cause and effect. They had to contractually absolve her from all of the responsibilities placed upon her by nature.

"Interesting way to put it," you may say.

Welcome to the world of closed-record adoptions. Only ten states currently have open records. At the time of the writing of this book, Illinois has just joined the list—and the crusade for basic human rights.

So this is a story about mountain climbing. This is a story about how it took an adopted child thirty years and thousands of dollars to learn what most people learn for free. This is a detective story, and a story about love. This is a story about mobsters and the FBI; about a child kept from knowing her past, and a woman named Lillie who could see the future.

This is a story about how I grew up in a tiny town, and studied and worked my way to become a prominent clinical psychotherapist, as well as clinical director of several venerable children's psychiatric hospitals.

This is a story about Oklahoma Governor Raymond Gary, whose name was being floated as a potential presidential running mate in 1955, and his friend, Averell Harriman, who visited him at the governor's mansion in Oklahoma City (photo page 214). It's a story about Randolph Churchill, who was in the United States reporting on the Democratic National Convention. He came through Oklahoma and visited the Officer's Club at Tinker Air Force Base where he met a woman named Irene Pruitt Gafford—whose DNA profile I would be handed in an envelope more than fifty years later.

This is a story about how I located my birthmother, and (without any warning) knocked on her front door in Purcell Oklahoma, fifty-two years after she handed me over to the state. This is a story about the child Irene Gafford conceived with Randolph Churchill—a story about Winston Churchill's granddaughter.

This is the story of…

Me.

"Your father was the black sheep

of the family. He drank.

Always up to no good.

Your grandfather was hoppin' mad

when he found out about you.

You could open a history book

and there he would be.

He was a famous man."

———

*Lillie, 1981*

# *"The chain of destiny"*

T o begin my life with the beginning of my life, I record that I was born (as I have been informed and
believe) on a Friday, at twelve o'clock at night. It
was remarked that the clock began to strike, and I began to
cry, simultaneously."

That is how one of the most famous characters in English
literature began the story that would determine whether he
would turn out to be the hero of his own life. To begin the
story of my own life, I report (as I have been informed and
believe) that I was born on Sunday, July 8, in the year 1956.

I do not believe my first appearance in the world was greeted with a clock's chimes, but like David Copperfield, the day and
hour of my birth would later be declared by a sage who would
take a lively interest in me. Also like Copperfield, whether I
should turn out to be the hero of my own life or whether that
role would be played by somebody else, these pages must show.

The week of my birth was not short of global news. Earth-
quakes and tidal waves struck a dozen Aegean islands south
of Greece and swept across the sea to the Turkish coast; a
vodka-soaked Nikita Khrushchev insulted almost everybody
within earshot at a party in Moscow; and Secretary of State
John Foster Dulles challenged Russian leaders to liberate
their satellite countries from "grievous captivity" to prove
the sincerity of their anti-Stalinist policies.

That same week in the United States, Governor W. Averell Harriman of New York complained about Republican use of "smear tactics" to suggest that Democrats were soft on Communism. He then charged President Dwight D. Eisenhower with being "very naïve" about the Soviets. Stan (The Man) Musial of the St Louis Cardinals was named player of the decade, followed by Joe DiMaggio of the Yankees and Ted Williams of the Boston Red Sox.

In the world of entertainment, Natalie Wood, perhaps Hollywood's most outstanding ingenue, offered beauty tips to young girls; the French singer Edith Piaf and Jacques Pills ended their marriage; Vivien Leigh and Sir Laurence Olivier announced they were expecting their first child after 16 years of marriage; John Wayne signed a three-picture deal at 20th Century Fox; Ed Sullivan booked Elvis Presley for three episodes of his TV variety hour; and the hit shows on Saturday night were *The Honeymooners*, *Gunsmoke*, and *Lawrence Welk*. It was into this strange mid-fifties admixture of bucolic Americana and Cold War paranoia that I was born, and the circumstances surrounding my entrance into the world were equally intriguing.

Probably most of you were in a hospital on the day you met the people who raised you. I was introduced to my family in a random hotel room near the state capital. But to best set the scene, we need to go back a little further, and meet the Noonans.

Jeanlee Noonan is my mom. She moved to Tonkawa, Oklahoma in 1926, when she was six weeks old. Her father, Howard Harold, had resettled his family there from Russell, Kansas, in order to take a job as a math instructor at Northern Oklahoma Junior College.

Tonkawa was a booming oil town in those years. Its population had soared to almost ten thousand, yet it retained a rough-and-tumble frontier spirit—with even an occasional gunfight on Grand Avenue.

In the early twenties, oil rigs had spread across the area like a swarm of gigantic mechanical mosquitoes bespeckling the landscape, piercing the oil rich soil and drinking up its petroleum by the barrelful. Intoxicated by the new infusion of cash fueled by the extraction of black gold, Tonkawa swelled and stretched out its sleepy lanes—welcoming two new drugstores, three grocery stores, several hardware stores, and even a few upscale clothing shops.

Along with the thriving businesses, it was rumored that some of the people in this small town—and in my own neighborhood!—were mob-affiliated; however my father, Jim Noonan, never spoke of it. I've always thought that the "Tonkawa Mafia," as they were called, was a term used lightly for a group that may have been involved in bootlegging and prostitution during the oil boom. However, there is a well-known story about a man named Sam Dixon who owned a Ford dealership in town, commonly known as "the Ford garage." It is said that a car belonging to the bank robber Pretty Boy Floyd was brought into Sam's dealership for repair, full of bullet holes, with the order that it be fixed and out in twenty-four hours. The boys at the garage were said to have worked all night long to make sure that happened.

My grandparents knew Sam's parents and were friends with them, so the story may have been true. But even if there was validity to this and other stories about organized crime, it never impacted my childhood in Tonkawa, aside from the excitement and nervous giggles shared with my friends at the possibility that we knew people in "the mob."

While Tonkawa was not a big city, it was home to a diverse group of people and was the center of much activity and prosperity. My mom's parents, Howard and Doris "Marie" Harold, flourished in this small, thriving community. Howard was a graduate of the illustrious University of Chicago. He had electric hazel eyes that never strayed, and ears that never failed to pick up a joke. He was a physically active man who golfed, bowled, and played tennis regularly. He was a professor in the college's mathematics department, and was known for his scintillating intellect and love for his students—whom he welcomed on the doorstep of his home when they turned up needing assistance with math problems. He was as passionate and animated while arguing the virtues of the Guatemalan Constitution of '56 as he was pondering Fermat's last theorem.

Howard Harold rose to the position of dean, and ultimately held the office of president of the college (where, to this very day, stands a building named Harold Hall in his honor). He was also a leader in the masonic lodge, where he forged countless friendships over the years, so that he grew to become very well known in the community—eventually accepting an invitation to sit on the Oklahoma State Board of Regents, where he met and worked with some of the most influential people in the state. He was also elected grand master of Masons for the state of Oklahoma.

A well-respected man, Howard cultivated a friendship with Raymond Gary, the governor of Oklahoma. They were colleagues on the Board of Regents for many years. Gary was also a friend and colleague of Averell Harriman, who had served as President Roosevelt's special ambassador to Winston Churchill from 1941 to 1944, and who had since become governor of New York. Harriman had asked Gary to run his campaign should he be nominated by the Democratic Party as a presidential candidate, which led to speculation that Gary might be selected as Harriman's running mate. As it turned out, the party endorsed Adlai Stevenson instead. But as you can imagine, "one of our own" as a possible vice-presidential candidate was the source of great excitement in Oklahoma at that time.

My grandmother Marie, was outgoing, well liked, and very well respected in Tonkawa. She was a volunteer for the Red Cross, worked for Associated Charities, and was active in Eastern Star, the American Legion, the Faculty Wives Club, and the Daughters of the American Revolution. While committed to these activities, she managed to raise three children as well: my mom, Jeanlee; my Aunt Jo (her twin sister); and my Uncle Bill. Marie was also a seamstress and made all her children's clothes.

Marie Harold's yard was always well manicured and was known for its profusion of flowers, fruit trees, and a working garden that fed our family and even some friends. This generation survived the Great Depression and was very proud of the life that it had managed to salvage from the wreckage of the late twenties. The Harolds were not wealthy by any means, but their standing in their small town established them as part of the "upper-crust."

Unfortunately, even a town this diminutive was not small enough to hide from the horrors of World War II. My Uncle Bill became Tonkawa's first casualty. He was killed in the Battle of Sunda Strait while serving on the USS *Houston*. On February 28, 1942 the ABDA *Perth* and *Houston* both steamed into Banten Bay, near the northern tip of Java, Indonesia. Apparently due to faulty intelligence, they were unaware that Japanese warships were waiting in the bay. The two ships evaded nine torpedoes launched by the destroyer *Fubuki*, but a Japanese destroyer squadron blockaded the Sunda Strait, placing the cruisers in the direct lines of fire of more than ninety Long Lance torpedoes. *Houston* and *Perth* could not withdraw. *Perth* came under fire at 23:36 and was sunk in less than an hour. *Houston* fought on alone until shortly after midnight, when she was hit by a Long Lance and began to founder. Still she fought on valiantly—landing hits on three Japanese destroyers, and sinking a minesweeper.

Three more torpedoes hit *Houston* in rapid succession. Captain Albert Rooks was killed at 00:30 as the ship came to a halt. Japanese destroyers closed in quickly, strafing the decks with large machine-gun fire. Only minutes later, *Houston* sank—en-sign still flying. Of the 1,061-man crew, 368 survived. Uncle Bill may have been killed at any time in the battle, but my grandmother would be forever haunted by images of Japanese warships slaughtering hundreds of soldiers on the deck of *Houston* as she sank. Uncle Bill was posthumously awarded the Purple Heart, and the crew of *Houston* is now honored alongside that of *Perth* at the Shrine of Remembrance in Melbourne, Australia.

Uncle Bill's death devastated Marie. The proverbial spark that leaves people in the aftermath of a trauma, departed from her in an instant, or perhaps was smothered by the heavy cloud of grief that descended after the news of his death. (As a child, she and I spent countless hours on her front porch overlooking Main Street, and I remember quite vividly—as I would teeter my way back and forth across the top of the railing—how she sat on the porch swing, staring into the middle distance with a drawn, spectral gaze.) Her anguish after Bill's death was often compounded by the shattering sound of Nazis marching down Main Street in Tonkawa.

Perhaps you thought my use of "Nazis marching down Main Street" was just a metaphor, or a reference to my grandmother's nightmares. But in fact this was one of the chilling realities of World War II. German and Italian prisoners of war were scattered throughout POW camps in Texas, Oklahoma, and Utah. My hometown was the site of Camp Tonkawa, which was in operation from August 30, 1943 to September 1, 1945, and which held thousands of POWs, including many high-ranking Nazis.

The first prisoners arrived in August 1943. Everyone in Tonkawa remembers the event with chilling clarity. My mom, Jeanlee, ran out to my grandmother's front porch as the train ground to a halt in downtown Tonkawa, and U.S. Army guards marched hundreds of prisoners down Main Street to the internment camp. Mom distinctly remembers the ground-shaking sensation of the soldiers' pounding feet as they approached—staring fixedly ahead—never daring to glance left or right at all the locals who gathered to bear witness. At the camp, the prisoners were put to work at local farms and ranches, running alfalfa dryers and doing other general labor. Camp Tonkawa became the site of a famous Nazi POW story. In November 1943, a prison riot was sparked by the death of a German soldier named Johannes Kunze, who had been a gefreiter in the Afrika Korps. Following a kangaroo court "trial" on November 4, 1943, he was executed for treason by his fellow POWs, eight of whom escaped into the Oklahoma countryside.

The evidence that Kunze was actually an American spy was obtained by the other POWs quite by accident. Kunze had been in the habit of passing information to the U.S. doctor during sick call. His notes contained information about the activities of high-ranking Nazis in the camp.

One day a new doctor was on duty who didn't know Kunze was a double agent and who couldn't read German. Kunze handed over the note, and the American doctor unwittingly blew his cover by sending it back through another POW, who read it and realized Kunze was a spy. News spread, and Kunze was quickly killed inside the camp by other prisoners.

In a fascinating side note, the Kunze case was prosecuted by Leon Jaworski, who would later reach national fame as the special prosecutor in the Watergate hearings. Jaworski prevailed in the case, and all five defendants were convicted and executed by hanging at U.S. Disciplinary Barracks, Fort Leavenworth, Kansas, on July 10, 1945. Their punishment had been delayed until after the end of the war due to fear of reprisals against U.S. prisoners held in Germany. The death of Johannes Kunze is the subject of a novel by Vincent S. Greene entitled *Extreme Justice*, and a nonfiction work by Wilma Trummel Parnell, *The Killing of Corporal Kunze*.

So, you didn't know Oklahoma was once crawling with Nazis? This is only the beginning of the story! But back to the story of my mom and dad.

Jeanlee Harold started noticing Jim Noonan when she was a junior in high school. Jim was a good man. This was written to a certain extent in his appearance; in his staid, brisk person, in his kind face, and extraordinarily decent demeanor, which told of steadfastness. They dated off and on; broke up a few times; then reunited when they discovered they were in love. But remember that the Harolds, although not wealthy, were the upper-crust of their small town, so they were not sanguine about the union. Howard believed Jim Noonan wasn't an appropriate match for his daughter.

But as time passed it became clear that Jeanlee deeply loved Jim, and perhaps reluctantly, the Harolds grew fond of their future son-in-law. In 1947, when Jeanlee was twenty-one years old, she and Jim married.

The Noonans enjoyed a happy and tranquil married life. Jim had a great job managing Taylor's, a farm implement store where they sold and repaired tractors and combines. Taylor's offered a valuable service to its farming community and the business was very successful. Jeanlee and Jim lived in a three-bedroom frame house with a fenced-in backyard. Both of their families lived nearby, which allowed for frequent get-togethers. Church friends were also a welcome part of their day-to-day lives—they would often meet at Linton's Steak House, which was known for its lamb fries, music, and busy dance floor. Socializing with friends and family was the source of most of the joy in their lives.

But there was something rather clearly, and quite painfully, missing. The Noonans didn't have a child.

So in 1951 they applied to the State of Oklahoma to adopt. Both of them understood that the process could be complex and protracted, but it didn't matter. They deeply wanted a child and were prepared to endure any amount of waiting or red tape necessary.

The first adoption interview took place in 1951 with a

placement worker for the Department of Human Services in Oklahoma City. Several additional interviews occurred over the next three years; then in 1953 a meeting was arranged with Lloyd Rader, the Director of Social Services. This was facilitated by my grandfather's good friend and neighbor, Ralph Cookson, who worked with both Rader and Governor Gary.

The interview went as well as the Noonans could've hoped. They learned that the process could be lengthy and they must be patient—but this was more easily borne with the newly strengthened hope of starting their own family.

Another year passed. Nothing. In 1954 a caseworker showed up for a home visit, and found everything in immaculate order. Their house, lifestyle, and marriage were poised for parenthood as they anxiously anticipated the joyful laughter and tears of a new baby. Surely now such joy was imminent.

Nothing.

Another quieter and seemingly longer year passed. The stress and sadness started to take its toll on the young couple. Anticipation, excitement, disappointment, and despair fused into one desperate emotional state. It was the not knowing that haunted Jeanlee most. DHS workers would call her without any notice. She had to leave work, go home, meet with them, then return to her bank job. And still nothing. This happened again, and again, and again. In the meantime a couple at church had adopted a boy. It seemed to work for other people in Tonkawa, but not for the Noonans. A DHS worker would come by and rekindle the hope and anticipation, and again...nothing. Countless times the Noonans were disappointed when a child was declared "not a good fit." They felt that it couldn't have anything to do with the type of home, care, financial support, or love that they could give a child. All of that was in order.

Then, on an odd spring day in 1956, the Federal Bureau of Investigation showed up in Tonkawa. Agents interviewed Harold and Marie, Fred French (Jeanlee's boss at the bank),

J. Morgan Bush (her former boss at a pharmacy), and a man named J.E. "Bus" Roberts. Bus was the owner of a local insurance company and influential businessman in the community. News of the FBI asking questions of locals spread like brushfire through the tiny town. Everyone who spoke to them said the agents were courteous and friendly, but no one could quite grasp what they wanted.

Finally, in the autumn of 1956, Jeanlee was so disillusioned with the entire adoption process that she told the caseworker so, in no uncertain terms. "No, this is it! I'm done! I've gone through this long enough and I don't want you to bother me anymore. It's all just politics and red-tape anyhow. Don't bother coming back again. It's the same ol' thing over, and over, and over. Nothing has changed since the last time you were here!"

And with those words she felt like she forfeited all the hope she ever held for having her own child. Jeanlee was devastated, and her pain was only intensified by the anticipation of the approaching holidays. She and Jim buried themselves in work and friendships.

It was a late-November evening. The giant Oklahoma sky was chilly and gray as the Thanksgiving holiday approached, and the Noonans' hearts were heavy. Their Chevy sedan wended its way through the expanse of farmland just outside of town. Jim held the wheel and stared at Jeanlee. They had often cheerfully driven this route to the home of their closest friends, Ernie and Eleanor Melichar, for an evening of cards. The Melichars lived in a small but warm and well-appointed house at the edge of their vast wheat farm. These card games had become a tradition over the years—in a place where traditions were the glue that held together a collage of friendships.

"Are you okay, honey?" asked Jim on the drive to the Melichars. "You're awfully quiet tonight."

"I was thinking about what a wonderful life we have together, except for not having a child. Now that I've told the adoption agency to forget it, I feel a little hopeless. I want a baby so bad Jim. I love our life, but I never saw it without children. Over the past week I've been so upset it's been almost unbearable."

Jim reached over and put his hand on Jeanlee's knee. "I know sweetheart. Maybe it just wasn't meant to be."

Jeanlee dreaded the possible truth of Jim's statement. They had tried unsuccessfully to conceive for years, and endured even more years at the mercy of "the system."

"Here we are, right on time," Jim said as he pulled up to the Melichars' house. "Let's just try to put all of this behind us for now and enjoy a good game of bridge."

And that they did.

Ernie and Eleanor were waiting for them. Jim and Ernie set up the card table and chairs while Eleanor and Jeanlee prepared goodies. They soon shuffled the cards, and fell into the comfortable conversation and card-playing they had grown to love.

At 9:30 the Melichars' phone rang. It was a call that would forever alter the course of the Noonans' lives. Eleanor called Jeanlee to the phone, explaining that her mother wanted to talk to her. But why would Marie call her this late, and at a friend's house? Jeanlee's heart pounded as she walked to the kitchen. She feared something was terribly wrong.

"Jeanlee," Marie said in a tremulous voice, "you have to go home right away and call the caseworker."

Jeanlee's heart stopped beating. "About what?"

"What else?" Marie said. "A baby."

"The FBI has always known
where you were.  It was a man's idea
to give you up for adoption.
Your grandfather didn't know
anything about it. They acted like
it was a disgrace. Your mother
was from a lower social circle
than your father. They thought she
was not worthy of him."

———

*Lillie, 1987*

# 2

## *"Ten thousand regulations"*

Jeanlee's heart started beating again as she realized her mother was talking about a possible adoption. "Go home and call? Why don't I just call from here?"

Marie was very firm in her response. "No. I told them I would have you call immediately, but they said very clearly that you must call from your *home phone*."

The Noonans and the Melichars thought this was an odd requirement, but the Noonans were so thrilled that they happily raced home. Jeanlee returned the call and was informed that there was a child available for placement, and that the proud parents-to-be could meet their new child the very next morning at eight o'clock sharp. They were given the address of a hotel near the capitol building in Oklahoma City, and instructed to let the desk clerk know when they arrived.

At 10 P.M., in the flurry of excitement that ensued, the expectant parents drove to Moore's dry goods store—and loaded the car with baby supplies: diapers, bedding, blankets, soap, toys, and bottles. The store owners, family friends, had agreed to open the store and met my parents-to-be. There would be a well-feathered nest for the new addition to their family.

The morning's drive to Oklahoma City seemed eternal, and the air was electric. At the hotel they were told there was a room reserved for them so they wouldn't have to wait in the lobby. They went to the room to wait. Jim alternated between pacing and sitting. Tick-tock. Tick-tock. Tick-tock. About thirty minutes passed.

In walked a woman—a caseworker, they assumed—and in her arms, the baby. Jim froze. Jeanlee held her breath. Never had the young couple seen a baby this beautiful. Never had they witnessed *any* sight this perfect. The caseworker handed the infant to Jeanlee, and in that very instant she felt the pain of years disintegrate into distant memories.

Jim and Jeanlee held their baby girl in their arms. I was a plump, round, tow-headed baby with chubby cheeks, in a yellow eyelet dress. I had cobalt-blue eyes and white hair.

"Thank God we got a little girl," said Jim. He had always wanted a girl.

And they were a family.

The Noonans soon settled into the rhythms of nascent family life: feeding, changing diapers, burping, rocking, feeding again. Some people find themselves with children they didn't expect or even want. Others may regard having children with some ambivalence—unsure of whether it's the right time, or how it will change their lives. Jim and Jeanlee fell into none of these categories. They had hoped, and worked, and waited so desperately for a child that they exulted in parenthood. Jeanlee was radiant. And now that the Noonans were a family, de facto, they were excited to become a family, de jure.

My legal life began before I was warmly welcomed into the loving arms of Jim and Jeanlee, when I was unceremoniously discarded from those of my biological mom—in a court of law. Most people will go their whole lives without appearing before a judge, but I was carried into court before I was old enough to crawl.

*July 17, 1956—In the Matter of the State in the interest of Baby Girl Gafford—PETITION:*

*Comes now Irene Gafford, a reputable person re-siding in Pottawatomie County, State of Oklahoma... and respectfully represents and states to the court that one Baby Girl Gafford born on July 8, 1956, in Pottawatomie County, Oklahoma, a child under the age of 16 years, is a dependent child in this to-wit:*

*That Baby Girl Gafford is the illegitimate child of Irene Gafford, petitioner...*

"Illegitimate." Ouch. I never understood that word. That was the same generation that styled people "lame," "retarded," and "crippled." But "illegitimate" has not yet been consigned to the politically correct ash heap of linguistic history where it belongs. I looked up "illegitimate" as a child, and found: "not authorized by the law; not in accordance with accepted standards or rules." This meant my existence was "not in accordance with accepted standards or rules." But then I got to definition 2: "born of parents not lawfully married to each other." Oh, so now it's my fault that my gene donors didn't walk down the aisle? They were the ones radically out of step with cultural norms, but I was the one who was branded from birth as inferior—and doomed to be so categorized for my entire life. But I digress from the legal proceedings (with the greatest of ease, and the least of reverence)...

*...that the petitioner has no home of her own and is not financially able to care for, nurture and educate said child at this time, and that by reason thereof said child is dependent upon the public for support; that petitioner believes it to be to the best interests of said child to place her in the custody of the Child Welfare Division of the Department of Public Welfare of the State of Oklahoma for care and maintenance, and for the purpose of finding a suitable home for adoption.*

Translation: "I am incapable of caring for or feeding my child, so I need to hand her over to the State of Oklahoma for care and feeding."

Hmmm...really? *Incapable?*

But maybe I'm bitter.

(I digress again.)

*Wherefore, Irene Gafford hereby voluntarily relinquishes all her right to, care and custody of, and power over said child, and prays that said child be made a ward of the court,...*

Yes, this is where she actually prays for someone to make her "indiscretion" disappear.

*...and that said child be committed into the custody of the Division of Child Welfare of the Department of Public Welfare of the State of Oklahoma for care and maintenance and for the purpose of finding a suitable home for adoption. That the said Irene Gafford resides at Shawnee, Oklahoma.*

By those words, written and filed on that date, the woman who gave birth to me was legally absolved of all responsibility for her actions—and for my life.

Also by those words, "Baby Girl Gafford" became my first name. I was abandoned on the steps of the state capitol—found floating in the reeds by a government employee. Of course, I have no memory of these first few months, but the psychological imprint would remain indelible throughout my entire life.

Obviously, my name is not Kim. But I am the same person described hereunder. How in the world my second name came to be Kim, I cannot tell you. It was an "alias," according to a note on my DHS file. How mysterious. This critique was the result of my first checkup when I was nine weeks old:

> *2.1 months—Techniques Used: Cattell Infant Scale; Griffith Developmental Scale—Kim is an unusual looking baby who has small wide-set eyes, an extremely narrow nose, and a large round face. She is a very chubby baby who has red hair, blue eyes, and fair skin.*
>
> *At this time Kim's motor development is satisfactory for her age, but she is somewhat unresponsive to sensory (visual) stimulation. Audition appears to be satisfactory, but her eyes do not yet seem to focus on objects within a close range. She can follow a moving person but does not seem to see something as small as a dangling ring. Since she is only 2 months old, this is not particularly significant at this time but will be observed when she is next seen for testing.*
>
> *INTERPRETATION: This is the first time that Kim has been seen for psychological testing, and she appears to be a healthy and well developed baby. Her progress is satisfactory in all areas except the visual. Here her ability to focus on objects at close range is slightly below average expectation, but it is much too early to attach any significance to this. Accordingly, she will be seen for further observation and testing next month. Cc: Polly Hunt*

Did he say "unusual looking"? "INTERPRETATION": I think he just called me ugly as tactfully as a physician should—considering it's part of the historical record. And who is Polly Hunt? Stay tuned...

I got my second checkup at eighteen weeks:

> *4.4 months—Techniques Used: Cattell Infant Scale; Griffith Developmental Scale—Kim continues to de-*

*velop in a consistent and satisfactory manner. Within the last month, she has become more attractive and her features do not appear as disproportionately small in relation to her large face as they did a month ago. Nevertheless, her face continues to be broad and her nose extremely narrow. In addition, she remains chubby and solid in build and appears to be healthy and strong.*

*Developmentally, Kim continues to progress at an average rate, although her pattern of growth is not altogether symmetrical. Graphically speaking, she reaches her peak of functioning in the locomotor area, maintains audition, vocalization, and personal-social responsiveness on an even plateau, and falls below her own mean in eye-hand coordination and manipulatory skills. This developmental deficit, however, is not significantly below the norm expected of her age, and constitutes a developmental pattern often characteristic of large and chubby infants.*

*INTERPRETATION: This is the third time that Kim has been seen for psychological testing, and her developmental pattern has been consistently within the average range. For purposes of permanent home placement, she can be considered of average ability, and will not be seen for further testing unless specifically requested.*

Did he say "more attractive"? Yet "not altogether symmetrical" and "characteristic of large and chubby infants"?

"INTERPRETATION": "She's not too bad looking for a fat alien-baby who has suffered a stroke." Don't these doctors know I'm going to read this someday? Have I really been dragged forth from nonentity into this squishy, breathing existence, only to be abandoned and insulted—before I even have teeth?

Thank God the cavalry—i.e. Jim and Jeanlee—was coming to the rescue:

*To the honorable Walter Doggett: Judge of the County Court of Kay County, Oklahoma.*

*Now on this 27th day of March, 1957, personally appeared before the County Judge of said County and State, James C. Noonan and Jeanlee Noonan, husband and wife and petition said Court for leave to jointly adopt as their own, baby girl Gafford, a minor female child of eight months of age, and to have the name of said child changed to the name of Rhonda Jean Noonan.*

*Said petitioners respectfully represent and state to the Court that they are adult persons, age 31 years and 30 years respectively and that they are husband and wife and are now living together as husband and wife and residents of Tonkawa, Kay County, Oklahoma, and that they have no child or children of their own.*

*Said petitioners represent and state to the Court that the said baby girl Gafford is the illegitimate child of Irene Pruitt and Robert Gafford and that their place of residence is unknown to petitioners; that said child has been legally placed in the care and custody of the Child Welfare Division of the Oklahoma Department of Public Welfare in care of Beverly Sutton, child welfare worker, post office box 1756, Ponca City, Oklahoma...*

Again with the "illegitimacy" stuff. At least the Noonans made it clear they were married—which everyone hoped would solve my legitimacy issues.

*That the said Irene Pruitt is one and the same person as Irene Gafford who appeared before the County Court of Pottawatomie County, Oklahoma, where she presented her petition, waiver of appearance, and consent to adoption of her child, baby girl Gafford and John L. Green, Judge of said Court entered an order on July 17, 1956 in case No. 1676 in said court, certified copies of said proceedings are herewith exhibited to this court for inspection and a photocopy is hereto attached marked exhibit "A" and made part of this petition.*

*Petitioners further represent and state that the Child Welfare Division of the Oklahoma Department of Public Welfare represented by Beverly Sutton, child welfare worker, who has the legal custody of said child and said minor child now appear before the County Judge of the said Kay County, Oklahoma, with each of your petitioners and are ready and willing to consent to the adoption by your petitioners and to the change of the name of said minor child to the name of Rhonda Jean Noonan.*

That the "said" Irene Pruitt is Irene Gafford...so which is it? These documents might be considered important by someone in the future. Is it Gafford or is it Pruitt? And what's the confusion—about your own name?

*WHEREFORE, your petitioners pray a speedy hearing of this petition and that they may be permitted to jointly adopt said child as their own and that the name of said child may be changed to Rhonda Jean Noonan. Dated this 27ᵗʰ day of March, 1957—James C. Noonan , Jeanlee Noonan.*

*CONSENT OF CHILD WELFARE DIVISION OF THE OKLAHOMA DEPARTMENT OF PUBLIC WELFARE—The undersigned has legal custody of the above named child, baby girl Gafford, and guardian of said child as provided by law, and does hereby consent to the hereinabove mentioned adoption of said child by James C. Noonan and Jeanlee Noonan, husband and wife. –Beverly Sutton.*

By those words, written and filed on that date, the man and woman who had already become my real parents, became legally obligated for my care and responsible for my welfare.

Also by those words, "Rhonda Jean Noonan" became my second name.

"Relatives will talk to you.
There are going to be tears.
Your grandfather made important
decisions. He was very smart. He could
say one word and everyone would
shut up. He didn't like the way you
were treated. Didn't know about it
until after it was done. He was
angry with your father. They had words
about it. He never forgot about you."

———

*Lillie, 1983*

## *"Intense simplicities"*

My childhood was pure Americana. I loved my neighborhood, even though I was almost the only girl. There was one other, but she was so much older that she didn't really count.

I had a whole herd of plastic horses—at least seventy-five. I collected them with the same vigor my grandmother collected pens. She also had an impressive collection of earrings from around the globe, courtesy of my Aunt Jo.

My love for horses became an acute condition when Aunt Jo sent a book called *Horses of the World*. I kept it in the toy drawer, and studied it assiduously.

When I was in the fifth grade Aunt Jo came to my school. I hadn't seen many people in uniform, so to see Aunt Jo in her Air Force attire struck me almost breathless. She did a slide show, and a room full of kids flew around the world without ever leaving Tonkawa. We were rapt: Holland, Switzerland, Turkey, France, etc. I didn't see Aunt Jo again until she retired, but she remained a vital presence in my life, despite being always on the other side of the world.

Aunt Jo was responsible for sending me the most magical things from the most mysterious lands; a Nikon camera from Germany, a camel saddle from Turkey, silver objects, little toy elves, figurines, beer steins, and a collection of fancy German Christmas-tree ornaments that rivaled those of any tree in Tonkawa. Every gift from Aunt Jo brightened my eyes.

We had a good-sized backyard. It was ringed by a cyclone fence and boasted a large mimosa tree. That tree was the main event in the yard, and I had a sandbox which sat under it. I would go out back, Mom would shut the gate, and I would play in the sandbox. She would monitor me from the kitchen window.

For a while she grew frustrated with me because I kept opening the gate and running up the alley to see what I could find. I was only about two years old at the time, much too young to wander alone outside the fence. As soon as she saw me take off down the alley, she would run out to catch me. My inevitable collaring and trip back to the yard was punctuated with a couple of swats. Mom would then implement some inventive re-rigging of the gate latch apparatus to prevent my next escape. She'd leave me to play, walk back up the three steps to the house, and by the time she got back to the kitchen window, I would be out of the gate and headed back down the alley.

Once my dad came home from work and Mom was expressing her exasperation with the miniature Houdini she was apparently rearing. My dad said, "If you would just latch that gate really well, she couldn't get out!"

"Okay, smartie, you go right ahead and show me how," replied Mom.

Dad went out to the gate and latched it to his satisfaction. He then turned around, walked back up to the house, and into the kitchen—where Mom said, "You better go back out and get your daughter—she's headed down the alley."

That became the metaphor for my life. My ardent, searching insistence and persistence would mark my next five decades.

The halcyon days of Tonkawa were spent in activities that were standard to 1960s America. When we weren't playing inside the house we were playing outside the house, and when weren't playing we were captivated by television. *Captain Kangaroo* was a mainstay, as was *Roy Rogers*. My young imagination would travel from *Petticoat Junction* to *Green Acres* and *Gilligan's Island*. We also loved *Bewitched* and *I Dream of Jeannie*, but my favorite was, of course, *The Lone Ranger*.

Oh, how I loved *The Lone Ranger*.

For years I desperately wanted a horse just like Tonto's. Until one day, a day I'll never forget, I saw John Wayne astride an Appaloosa. "Wow," I said. I knew then and there I had to have an Appaloosa.

In spite of all this, the cold, hard fact of my adoption was never far from my mind. I remember at school we were assigned to write papers about our ancestry. The teacher held a long discussion about where all of our families had come from—England, Ireland, Italy, Germany, etc.

Where did *I* come from?

I was haunted by the question—fixated on it—and pondered it incessantly. A few days later I was at Gran's house; I thought I would put the same question to her, and see how she answered.

"I'm English and Irish," Gran said.

"But what am I?"

"You're the same thing I am," she claimed.

"No, I'm not." I knew I wasn't the same as she was, and I assumed she knew it too. I pressed her further. "Do people ever look for their real parents?"

"You wouldn't want to do that," she said at once, and I knew by the celerity of her response that she was uncomfortable with the entire subject.

But this was another gate I refused to leave latched—an alley I could not leave unexplored. I persisted. "Who are my real parents?"

"We know almost nothing about them," said Gran; and she went on to state that my father was "high up in the government" and was killed in a car wreck on his way back to Washington, and that my mom was a beautician.

A few days later I got a little more information out of her. We were back on the porch, and she recounted what my adoption caseworker had said: "If you were told the name of the baby being given up for adoption, you would know immediately who it was…they are famous."

This was the first insinuation of a name of renown in my family tree.

"I didn't ask any questions," Gran continued, "because I just wanted things to go smoothly for your parents." It made sense that the caseworker had given her this strange piece of gossip, because Gran actually knew her—they had known each other for years.

I took it easy on Gran, probing only far enough into matters so that I didn't offend or excite her—backing off when I got too close to a nerve, then quietly pursuing my quest without a whisper of my curiosity. I knew she never wanted me looking for my biological parents, but I never really understood why. I often reassured her: "It wouldn't make any difference who I found, you'll always be my grandma."

And Gran in turn was always flattering me: "I don't know what I would do without you…you're the light of my life." This warmth and connectedness was reassuring to me as a child.

Mom enjoyed the joyful shock of her first pregnancy when I was five years old. At first no one believed it. Finally the doctor recommended Jeanlee take a pregnancy test. He called to announce that the rabbit had died.

Jim was as surprised as Jeanlee, if not more so; and he was equally thrilled about his growing family. My brother Jim was born, and soon after I started school. I waltzed right into kindergarten without a care or even a hesitation. I later learned it was much harder for Mom to leave me there than it was for me to be left.

I'm told that I was very social as a young child. My brother was more introverted. He could entertain himself for hours, even days, playing quietly on his own, whereas I seemed to require more external forms of amusement. We played all summer while Dad worked at the grain elevator. Harvest was his busiest time. Tonkawa was wheat territory. Harvest season started the first week in June—with equipment maintenance, repairs, preparations—and ran till November. My dad worked hard.

I felt my first stirrings of deep and abiding love for animals at this age. Ming entered my life when I was eleven. He was a great cat. We had a Ford Galaxy 500, and every day when Dad would come home from work, Ming would hide behind the car and lunge out and attack him, like Kato attacking Inspector Clouseau. It was a tradition. Ming was a tough cat, too. One day we heard some pitiful whimpering and whining coming from the garage. We ran out to discover that Ming had cornered a German shepherd under the car. Ming lived to be sixteen years old.

I didn't have traditional sleepovers at our house, because it was very small; in fact I shared a room with my brother. We became best friends; we spent what felt like thousands of hours playing outside. Spring brought out the green grass frogs, for which we would hunt tirelessly, day after day. The days seemed to blend together...all of them wonderful.

It was remarked that I was a perfectionist as a child. I was famous for taking everything apart that could be taken apart, and putting it back together with deft skill. My Bible School teacher said I drove her up the wall with it. This charge would echo through the forthcoming years. Perhaps my perfectionism drove my quest. Never a day passed that I didn't contemplate it—that I didn't wonder.

"Who."

"Am."

"I?"

It was never entirely out of my mind. Nor was it ever left

off the harassment menu with other kids. I was taunted and teased about being adopted. It was a small town; there was no way to escape people knowing about it. Every parent knew, and inevitably shared it with their own kids. They probably admonished them not to talk about it, or use it against me; but any such admonishments fell on grade-school ears. The other kids felt sorry for me—that my birthparents didn't want me. And, in fairness to plain old healthy curiosity, they also wanted to know what it was like—how it was different. Everyone knew they had a secret weapon if they wanted to hurt me.

There were only three adopted children in our entire circle of friends—John Street, Rhonda Lacey, and me. We were the three *adopted kids*. And we were never allowed to forget what that meant. I remember a neighborhood kid taunting me: "You don't have to mind those people you live with, they're not your parents!"

It stung. It burned in my ears like acid, and in my bones like potential truth. I knew the indictment was false in the metaphoric sense of "parents"—of course my mom and dad were my mom and dad—but I was haunted by its genetic truth.

I recall another time when I was playing jacks with a school acquaintance. Angry because I won a game, she said, "You don't even have any parents…your parents didn't want you."

I replied, "I may be adopted, but I make straight A's and you are dumb." I knew she struggled in school and I had leveled the playing field.

My mom knew the teasing bothered me, too. But much to her credit, she remained as staunch in her honesty as she was in her clarity. "We've always been open and honest," she said, "and explained to you that you were adopted. That means we *chose* you. We picked you. We had to move heaven and earth to get you."

It helped, certainly. But it didn't stop the occasional juvenile haranguing and subsequent humiliations. Someone had told my mother that the roughest year for an adoptee is the second grade, and she may have been right. I could drift into quite comfortable states of semi-denial for brief and peaceful interludes, but then the kids in our community were capable of bringing me right back to reality with one verbal prick of a needle.

Holidays were magical and I spent much time with my mom's parents. Gran loved Easter, and she always dyed eggs with us. And we always had Easter baskets. Spring meant we could be outside even more, and barefoot. Our knees were stained with chlorophyll, and our days were filled with outdoor fun. There were years that came with a locust season, and boasted zillions of them. They sang their buzzing sounds through the endless, moist, halcyon days.

When the fruit trees bloomed, Mom would make a cherry pie and I would de-cherry it by popping the cherries out through the latticed top. I have always loved cherries. I remember watching Gran bake. She had lived through the depression and wasted nothing. Whenever the recipe called for an egg, she would crack the egg open, and run her index finger in an arc through the inside of each remaining half-shell—just to extract every last drop of tasty egg goodness.

Remember, Gran lost her son Bill in the war, and it had practically crippled her. She just hadn't really been a complete person afterward. But then I came along and palliated her grieving. My presence in Gran's life seemed to fill a part of the space that had been missing since Uncle Bill died. Of course, nothing could ever fill all of it. No one is quite the same after losing a child.

I remember how much I loved being at my grandparents' house. When Granddad came home he would have a cocktail, and I would always get his maraschino cherry (I would eat two more for every one I vouchsafed into his glass). We would sit and watch $M*A*S*H$, and he would laugh by snorting, "Arf, arf, arf, arf!"

Not a summer passed that we didn't catch lightning bugs and ensconce them in a Mason jar. One summer I found a baby bat by the driveway. I attempted to return it to nature, by hanging it up in a tree. Have you ever seen a bat up close? That was the ugliest thing I'd ever seen as a child.

Midway through summer came the holiday technically called Independence Day, but I only ever knew it as "the fourth." The fourth was never just one day in my childhood summer; it lasted for weeks. Dad would drive us to the firework stand where we would load up on Roman candles, fountains, glow worms, black cats, and bottle rockets—and don't forget the punks!

We shot firecrackers as soon as we bought them, and kept shooting them till they stopped selling them. Usually we did this in the backyard, but sometimes we went down to the river. Dad would make hamburgers on the grill, and we would have watermelon, strawberries and shortcake, and homemade ice cream out of the old hand-crank ice-cream maker. Sometimes, at the river, a different kind of shot would ring out, as some boys hunted frog and toads with their rifles.

Tonkawa summers seemed far away from everything. Dusty vines overhung low-slung houses, and monotonous avenues of parched saplings drooped beneath a relentless sky. So did the horses, and so did the exhausted farmers in the fields. Everything that grew and breathed was oppressed by the scorching glare—except for an occasional lizard. The very dirt was fiery brown, and something heaved in the air as if the atmosphere itself were panting.

We walked barefoot in the grass, avoiding hot concrete or stone. To come out of the protective shade of trees and houses was like plunging your feet into a scorching river, and swimming for your life to the nearest strip of cooling shade. Summer could be both brutal and magical...sometimes at the same time.

Like most childhoods, mine was filled with enthusiasms, terrors, hopes, and disappointments.

All during my youth Saturday morning meant only one thing: cartoons. Tom & Jerry, Popeye, Bugs Bunny, Road Runner, Daffy Duck, Wile E. Coyote, Yosemite Sam, Mickey Mouse, Minnie, Goofy. Those were the bologna sandwich days—Kool-Aid, Fritos, *American Bandstand.*

Francis and Dale Jones lived catty-corner to us. They were Mom and Dad's bridge buddies. Francis often brought over the best yeast rolls I'd ever tasted, and her famous peanut-butter fudge. And "the cellar" was at their house. This was a moldy concrete hole designed to keep one safe during a tornado. But it concealed mostly dead spiders, and a rickety old spring bed with a feather mattress with blue ticking. The tornado warnings were frequent and we knew the drill: get on your galoshes and raincoats, and get into the "'fraidie hole."

When I was around ten, I saw a bicycle downtown that I desperately wanted, but it was sixty dollars. That was a fortune. Gran saved up the money, and I was so excited. We went down to Western Auto and we bought it. I was over the moon with joy. But I was just a kid, and didn't realize the rules of preferential and reciprocal treatment of siblings. Dad got home from work, parked by the street, and I rode over to show him my new bike.

He was *not* amused as my brother Jim didn't get a new bike.

Naturally, his disapproval just devastated me. I was so thrilled and so proud, and had looked forward to showing it to him with such eager anticipation. His response made me want to crawl in a hole and disappear. At that point, I didn't even want the bike anymore.

Mom assured Jimmy, "We'll get you a new bike when you get older."

"I can take Sissie's hand-me-down," he said.

Jimmy's retort left me feeling like a piece of crap. All the joy was sapped from the entire event.

Mom was an excellent seamstress. She did quite a bit of sewing back then. I once fell in love with a pattern I saw—a dark purple field with big, bright dappled colors. Mom bought several yards of it and made me a very nice jumper based on one I had seen and liked. I made the mistake of visiting Grandma and Grandad Noonan's house in that jumper. When I was leaving to walk back home, Grace Noonan said, "That makes her look like a clown!" I would like to say she thought I was out of earshot, or that her voice was just too loud, but I believe she knew I could hear. I heard the peals of laughter that followed.

Grandad Noonan always sat in the den at my aunt and uncle's house. As a general rule of thumb I avoided going in there as much as possible, because I knew he would be sitting in there. I would swelter in 105-degree dust-bowl heat for hours without refreshments just to avoid passing him in the den. It was easier to rehydrate with the garden hose than deal with his angry comments.

I remember working at the stable of my dad's brother-in-law, Uncle Bill, and being so proud of my progress that I came in the den to announce to Grandad Noonan that "I just about have the one horse where I can ride it!"

"Oh, that horse is just gonna kick your stupid head off."

Ouch. Grandfather Noonan also took several occasions to remind my mom that I "wasn't blood." I suppose what appears in retrospect to be venomous hatred might have been mere ignorance and disrespect. But as I child I couldn't grapple with those nuances, so it burned like fire in my consciousness. I did not understand why they didn't like me.

Dad's sister, my Aunt Juanita, lived on the edge of town with Uncle Bill; he wore a cowboy hat and boots and he was an auctioneer. I remember playing by the hour in the garage with an antique parade saddle Bill had purchased. I was mesmerized. It was huge. The smell of leather and horses was perfection.

I imagined riding across the plains, and dreamed of having my own horse one day. I played with that saddle for months. Being an auctioneer seemed to me to be the most splendid, exotic profession in the world.

At that same auction Bill bought two Shetland pony mares that were pregnant. When they foaled, there were two mares and two babies. I named the palomino filly "Misty." Bill kept them at his house so I could ride them all around his and Juanita's ten acres.

There were basically two restaurants while I was growing up: Mary's Tonkawa Grill on Grand Avenue, and Linton's Steakhouse. Mary's offered homemade classic American fare: yeast rolls, cinnamon rolls, chicken fried steak, fried chicken, pot roast, pork chops, and so on.

Linton's Steakhouse was a supper club. It was famous for lamb fries and onion rings. Every Saturday night Mom and Dad went to Linton's, so a babysitter would come to watch us, and we got a choice of our own dinner: Dairyland or Tastee Freeze. Dad would bring us whichever dinner we wanted, and then head to Linton's with Mom.

Summers gently gave way to autumns, and Halloween blew in. We went trick-or-treating on a three-block area near our home. Then we climbed into the car and were taken to houses of friends who lived farther away.

The holidays reached full swing by Thanksgiving. Family time was at our house, with turkey, stuffing, canned cranberries, homemade rolls from Francis Jones, mashed potatoes, turkey gravy, and stuffing with giblets. There was never alcohol, and we never ate on the good china—not even on holidays. The TV presided over the living room. On Thanksgiving Day the sounds and images of the Macy's parade provided the backdrop to our merrymaking.

I often looked forward to church because my attendance

was rewarded with cinnamon rolls from Mary's Tonkawa Grill, pleasantly sweetening an otherwise bland ritual for Presbyterian children. I can still smell those rolls; their aroma permeates my memories of church. From sixth to twelfth grade I had a female pastor, Betty Knott, whom I admired very much; she was an additional reason to like the services.

I only remember one Christmas when it snowed, but the flakes didn't linger long enough to style it a "white Christmas." Almost as sacred as Christmas itself was the requirement for a real tree. Mom and Dad had a synthetic silver tree, but Grandma and Grandad wouldn't dream of such a thing. They took us to Dorsett's IGA to buy a live tree, and Gran, directing the affair from her recliner, would tell us exactly how to decorate it.

Till this day, the sounds of *A Charlie Brown Christmas* or *Rudolf the Rednosed Reindeer* send me spiraling back to those Christmases of my youth. I even sold Christmas cards door-to-door when I was twelve.

Mom baked her famous pies, and we made peanut brittle and trays of Christmas cookies with all the yuletide icings and sprinkles—balls and bells and stars and reindeer and snowmen—all in gingerbread. We ate peppermint candy canes and sat up late watching the local weatherman, Don Woods, track Santa's sleigh on his tornado radar, while our stockings hung expectantly on the hearth.

I loved Christmas. One year I got a guitar and a tennis racquet; another year, a microscope-and-slide kit. I made my own slides with the microscope kit. Christmas meant New Year's Eve was days away. We watched Dick Clark and stayed up till the ball dropped, and no New Year's Day was complete without the Rose Bowl parade.

As I got older, my adopted status would bubble up here and there. Going to the doctor's office, I would inevitably be subjected to questions like, "And does such-and-such run in your family?"

Awkward pause.

Parents call a huddle.

Grown-ups whisper briefly.

Then they all break from the huddle and cast a knowing and compassionate look in my direction.

I became a better and better cook as I grew up. My specialties included chocolate chip cookies, homemade pizza, and the best chicken-fried steak in the known world. Gran had a peach tree. When the succulent fruits were ready for canning, Gran would engineer an assembly line and we would can all the peaches.

I played a little basketball and hung out with the nerdy and offbeat kids; one year I worked on the yearbook. My friend Mike McAnally was locally famous in the area for the time a flying saucer landed in his family's pasture. I found him totally fascinating and listened, enthralled, to the tale.

At fifteen-and-a-half I got my drivers permit, and I got my license at sixteen (even though I wouldn't get a car until eighteen). I loved driving.

I went to junior prom with Mark Moorman, and to senior prom with Pete Scott. I got good grades, had some very good friends, and made some cherished memories. But never far from my mind was the desire to pursue my goal—to find out where I came from.

"There will be pictures and stories about who you are. You will be in the newspaper. People will want to talk to you and your family will want you to be quiet. They want it kept a secret. The man on your birth certificate is not your father. They will tell you he is, but he is not. I can tell you when this will happen…it will happen during the time of the colored money. They will put pretty colors on our paper money. That's when this will happen."

———

*Lillie, 1984*

**4**

# "A riddle wrapped in a mystery inside an enigma"

I graduated from Tonkawa High School in December of 1973, even though I was in the class of 1974. Rather than sit around all winter wasting time, I enrolled in classes at Northern Oklahoma Junior College (where my grandfather, Howard Harold, had been a leader), and matriculated efficiently.

I drove a Mercury Monterey family sedan and my college buddies and I spent many an evening haunted house hunting in wheat fields all over the countryside. Abandoned farm houses provided a spooky fun source of entertainment and sense of adventure.

At Northern Oklahoma I was always proud to walk by the building named for my grandfather: Harold Hall. After earning an Associate's degree I moved to another Oklahoma town called Stillwater, home of Oklahoma State University.

Being an excellent tennis player, I had been promised an athletic scholarship by the coach. But when I went to the athletic director's office, no one knew anything about it. The coach was finishing her doctorate, they told me, and was on leave to write her dissertation.

Since nobody there knew anything about it, they said, "Just show up to tryouts."

I did. I won both of my matches handily...and was not invited back. I was sad and angry.

I endured only a few months there because I was miserable and lonely. I didn't have any friends in Stillwater. I'll never forget walking into my chemistry class for the first time to discover there were three hundred people in an auditorium. That was overwhelming to me. I didn't want to be there. I realized I was only there to play tennis, and if I couldn't do that, I didn't want to be there at all.

I leveled with my mom and dad, confessing how miserable I was there, how suffocating and depressing it was. I told them I was thinking about other places to go, and that Tahlequah and Northeastern State University sounded nice. I relocated there, which proved one of the best things I ever did.

The week I arrived it snowed fourteen inches, covering everything. There were four of us in the dorm, having arrived early before classes began, and we became fast friends. Even though I had just arrived in town (exactly like Stillwater, not knowing anyone), within a week I was forging some very strong friendships. Maybe being snowbound helped.

I struggled like all middle-class youngsters to pay for school. I secured a tennis scholarship and it helped a little, plus I was granted ten hours a week of work study; and Mom was working at the donut shop, where she made about seventy-five dollars a week. She sent it all to me. And I was able to play competitive tennis, which I would do for three years.

After Tahlequah and a teaching degree, I moved to Tenkiller Lake on Cookson Bend. The house literally sat on a rock bluff, with an electric lift that went down to the lake. I would come home from school and take the lift down the hill, jump into a boat, and take off across the water. I also had a motorcycle which I quite enjoyed.

I took a job at Muskogee High School, which had three thousand students. I taught grades ten and eleven. Muskogee had a really active tennis community, in which I thrived. Also, my teaching degree allowed me to instruct driver's education. So I taught young drivers, and coached the two tennis teams. Teaching occupied four hours a day, and I coached for the balance of the day.

I was a bit of a trailblazer; in fact, I was the only female 5A coach in the state of Oklahoma at that time (1979-80 and 1980-81). I finished my second school year there and found myself restless—anxious to move forward with my life and career. I knew I wouldn't be a teacher all my life, so what was I waiting for?

I moved to Tulsa and lived with a friend of mine from graduate school, Cindy Sutton. She had a wonderful house in the middle of town and plenty of room.

One Saturday, Cindy suggested that we go to a tiny town called Cleveland to visit her mother's great aunt, Lillie. She explained that Lillie was a palm reader, and asked if I had ever enlisted the services of anyone like that.

"No," I said, "but I'll ride along."

We climbed into Cindy's heather-green '78 450 SL Mercedes and departed.

Cleveland evoked memories of Tonkawa; it was typical middle America. Cindy parked at a small house on a nondescript street. It was a safe bet that anyone who knocked on the front door didn't know Lillie, because everyone who knew her just entered through the back door—as we did now.

We entered into a sun room which had been converted into a makeshift TV parlor. A very pleasant, elegant looking elderly woman greeted us. She had the most beautiful long, white hair swept up on her head. Her eyes sparkled and she smiled easily. Although the passage of time had aged her, it had not hidden the fact that she had been a beauty. I was captivated by her sweet personality and sense of humor.

We sat down with her, and Cindy asked if she would read her palm. Lillie obliged. I stayed in the TV room, which was full of wicker furniture cushioned with floral-print pillows. A metal TV stand supported a tiny television set which was tuned to a western movie, and it was LOUD. Lillie loved westerns—especially John Wayne (whom she had met). A wicker couch and a recliner were the largest pieces of furniture, and the couch boasted a matching coffee table.

Cindy returned from her reading with a startled look on her face. She started telling me piecemeal what she had heard, and was trying to contextualize it, but I was more focused on how the experience had affected her; she was so energized. She suggested I go for a reading. I initially had no intention of doing so, but I cannot deny that seeing her response piqued my curiosity.

So I agreed. I didn't believe there was anything to that kind of stuff, so I thought I would just congenially abide the process, and discreetly roll my eyes should anything nonsensical happen. Cindy sat down in the TV room, and I entered the reading room.

There was a miniature table with a built-in elbowed dentist's light. Chairs bookended each side of the table. It fit very much into the stereotype of a "grandma's house." A cat calendar adorned one wall, and on its opposite hung a cat-shaped clock which ticked away the minutes, and the hours, and the years of Lillie's life in this house.

I sat down and she said, "Can I see your hands?"

I obliged her.

"Let me look at your palms," she continued. The table was low enough so that you could comfortably rest your arms on it. Lillie's own hands had long and immaculately manicured fingernails, even at her age. She gently pulled my hands toward her, and I finally got close enough to see the depth of age and character in her face. Her hair was as white as snow—airy tendrils wrapped and piled like alto-cirrus clouds. The longer I studied her face, the less I could distinguish its individual features, and the more compelled I was by the entire portrait of this woman.

She drew her hand up over my palm, fixed her gaze on it, and began to tap it with two fingers.

*Tap, tap, tap, tap...*
Each finger followed a different line.

*Tap, tap, tap, tap...*
The same fingers would trace another line—tapping over it, skipping up and down on it, then changing course to follow another line. She focused her eyes and tapped some more, looked up with a dazzling stare, then ebbed into a former life, it seemed—lapsing far back in a mystical dream infused with imagery. She would speak occasionally, a fragment, and then *tap, tap, tap, tap...*a rhythmic, mesmerizing pulse.

It seemed like the cat clock had stopped. It seemed like the cat *calendar* had stopped. She held my palms open and now swiped back and forth across them, studying the lines, sweeping here, then study another, pausing to comment, then sweep there—forging a sort of broken language...a strange syntactic construction of things she saw.

She told me I would go back to school. I argued, insisting I wouldn't go back to school. She told me I wanted to live out in the country.

Then, said the sage, "I'm seeing your father and your father's dead."

"No, he's not dead."

"Yes."

"No."

"Yes."

"Oh, you mean my biological father?"

"Your father..."

She said my father did a lot of things that embarrassed my grandfather; that my father had been the black sheep of the family, and that one day I would know all about him. "Your grandfather loved you," she declared.

Wait, hold on a minute.

He loved me?? Someone in my biological family *loved* me?

For this adoptee, that changed *everything*.

I knew from that moment—that statement—that I had to find that person. It struck a chord deep inside. This quest for my genetic heritage had never been far from my mind, and this just added fuel to the fire of my desire to know.

"Really?" I asked Lillie.

"Yes," she replied. "He was angry about what was done with you."

I was blown away by the reading. As I rejoined Cindy, on the TV was an image of John Wayne astride an Appaloosa—the exact same image I saw as a child when I first decided I wanted an Appaloosa.

We got in the car and I started talking and didn't stop for forty-five minutes. I was revitalized, rejuvenated—recharged. This woman Lillie knew so many things. I started writing them all down as soon as I got home: she knew that I was adopted. She told me to focus on my heart. She knew Grandfather Noonan had been cruel to me. She knew I had one brother, and that he kept to himself—often on the periphery of the family. And she knew that my father struggled with alcoholism; not only my adopted dad, but my biological father. She asked me if I had ever struggled with alcohol, and I told her no.

The very atoms in the air seemed electrified. I knew that this woman Lillie knew what she was talking about. She also made a comment that my biological father's family felt as though my birthmother was not of their social class; that they felt he had gotten involved with someone who was not "worthy" of him. So much of what she said I knew to be right, and some of what she said was so meaningless, that I couldn't help wondering what future events would unfold to supply meaning to things that now appeared meaningless. I turned it over a million ways in my head, analyzed and reanalyzed it a thousand times. The one thing I knew for certain was that I had to hear more.

I had asked Lillie how she was able to read palms. She

said, "Honey, I just look at the lines and pictures come to me. I get ideas and try to describe what I feel."

I went back to the daily grind of my normal life, but Lillie was so eerily, shockingly, astonishingly right about some things, that I could not escape the pull her meeting had on my mind.

I couldn't stop thinking about it.

It wasn't long until I told Cindy I was going back, and did exactly that.

At the second reading Lillie again touched on the course of my career, saying, "You're going go back to school to do something totally different." As that was the last thing I wanted to do at that point, I argued with her a bit but she refused to reconsider her statement.

Lillie did not mince her words; nor did she always have happy news. I remember once I was in an incredible relationship that I really thought would be permanent—till death do us part. I was explaining to Lillie that I was quite happy, and really knew I would spend the rest of my life with this one.

"No." She tapped on my palm. "No, you won't."

*Ouch*, I thought. So much for wish fulfillment. I was deeply in love, and couldn't imagine it ending. But Lillie was unwavering: "This is not the one. You really can't trust the relationship."

And sure enough, it ended after eight years. I realized on quite a few occasions that Lillie said only what she saw, not necessarily what you wanted to hear.

The Oklahoma economy had tanked and I was looking for a new job. I had quit my teaching job after deciding teaching wasn't for me, and I didn't know what I wanted to do for sure. So I took on odd jobs while pondering and planning the direction of my life. I helped a friend who was a property manager for a while, and dabbled in entrepreneurship with a company called LiveWire that I owned with my friend Denna.

At the date of the writing of this book, I have known Denna and Harriet for thirty years. They are the sort of friends one has in one's life forever—fixtures, sort of like the church in Europe, or the mountains in Colorado; they permeate one's entire history.

I relied on my good friends for emotional support while still searching for the right career path, and I remember the time as being quite scary—not knowing what direction my life would go. I had been trying to get a job in Tulsa for almost a year, and couldn't find anything decent. I knew it wouldn't be easy, going a year without a job—the strain would be tremendous, the effort exhausting. The weeks continued growing into months, and finally I just made the decision.

I would go back to school, and become a therapist.

Lillie was right, again.

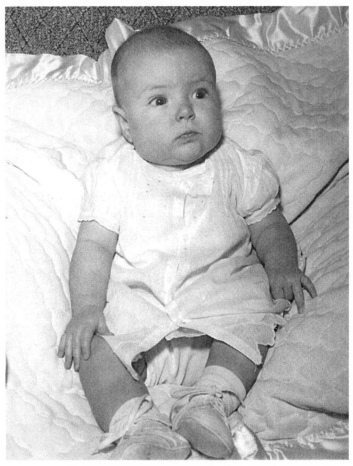

*This page: My first picture: four months old.*
*Opposite, top: Mom and Dad with me at four months.*
*Bottom: Grandpa and Grandma Harold with me.*

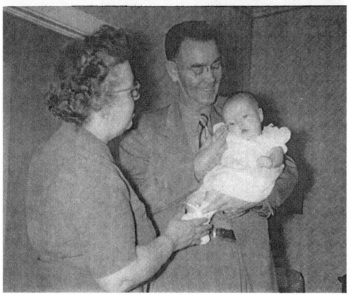

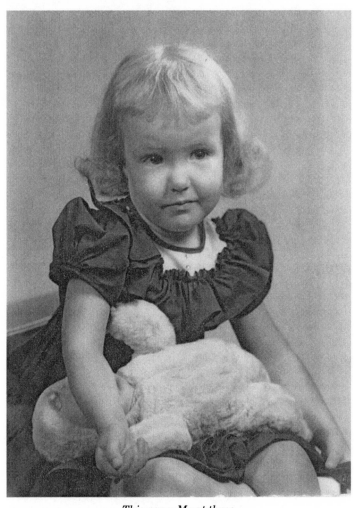

*This page: Me at three.*
*Opposite, top: I address the family.*
*Bottom: Backyard, age four.*

*This page, top: The family at my grandparents' 50th wedding
anniversary in 1970 (left to right: Jim, me, Dad, Mom,
Jo, Marie, Howard).
Bottom: Bubba and me in Colorado.
Opposite page: Lillie reads my hands.*

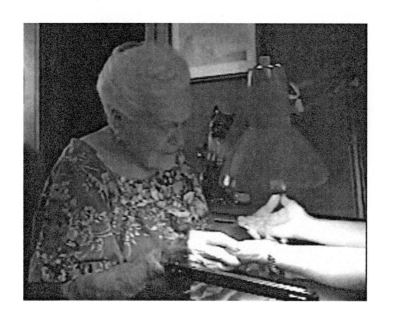

"You look like your father—through the cheekbones and eyes and mouth. They dread the day you are found. They will look you over good. You get your love of horses from your grandfather. He had many race horses and knew all their names."

———

*Lillie, 1988*

# "A measureless and perpetual uncertainty"

I had been back in school for a couple of years when the Director of Children Services at Shadow Mountain Hospital asked me to work on their children's unit. I was doing well in school, thoroughly enjoying the material, the concepts and the homework. I was also feeling a bit more certainty in my career trajectory, so I agreed to take the job.

I fell in love with it. It was a dream job. Not only was the work terrific, but I cultivated some deep and abiding friendships there as well. And, also very importantly, I learned that it was a lifestyle I could adjust to. I could handle the professional mental health services field. It was composed of good people who wanted to help others (heaven knows we weren't in it for the money). I arrived at work each morning with a smile on my face, even though I was exhausted from studying the night before. I finished my prerequisites and eventually started graduate school.

Part of the journey to becoming a therapist is to experience therapy. I decided to use the opportunity to work on some of the issues I had about being adopted. I felt I had a lot of grief and loss to deal with, because adoption had affected my personal life, love life, family life, and social interactions. Adoption reaches deep into the emotional core of everyone involved. So I started digging into my adoptive history with a therapist.

Much to my chagrin (if not horror), I began to realize that this therapist didn't know any more about adoption than I did.

In fact, he knew a whole lot less about it than I did. It struck me like thunder: I realized that therapists needed to understand that there is a very intricate dance that happens between what was typically considered an adoption issue versus what was identified as attachment symptomology.

In that therapist's room I suddenly knew I would finish school and devote my life to psychotherapy focusing on adopted persons. (Which proved my first therapy sessions were invaluable after all.) The experience jolted my ambition to study with an almost hyperthyroidal drive. I applied myself to the study of adoption and attachment with a ferocity previously unknown in my pursuits.

Whenever I could get away for a few hours, I went back to see Lillie. As time went on, I consistently heard the same stories from her. She told me I had been "left things," in response to which I explained that my family wasn't wealthy, and there was nothing to leave me. She said my grandfather has passed on, but his spirit is everywhere, and that he didn't know they were giving me away. She said my mother gave me up because they "fussed at her." And that she had two or three jobs, and practically worked herself to death. Lillie saw into my everyday life, she read my past, and she foresaw countless events in the future.

I worked and studied, and worked and waited, and couldn't sit still in my search to find my grandfather. Lillie's bizarre readings sounded unbelievable, but she knew so much about me that I came to take what she said very seriously. She told me that there were things "meant to happen." I wasn't sure what I should or could do to help things along, but I believed that a person should help herself. I decided to begin educating myself on adoption practices, and the processes followed to place me in my adoptive home.

I phoned the state capital to talk to the adoption unit at the Oklahoma Department of Human Services, and discovered it was run by a woman named Bonnie Walton. I wrote to ask her to pass on my information to the State Reunion Registry. For the registry to work, both parties—the adopted person and the parent—had to submit their information. So I wrote the letter, sent it on its way, and hoped I would hear something.

Days passed.

Then a week.

Finally a letter arrived on January 3, 1983.

*Dear Ms. Noonan:*

*We are in receipt of your letter in which you state you are an adult adoptee and that you are interested in finding your biological mother and brothers and sisters. You will be interested to know that this agency has a registry by which adult adoptees and biological family can register if they wish to find each other. When the requests match up, the agency can assist in a reunion. We have checked our registry to see if your biological mother or your brothers and sisters have come forward wanting to find you; however, they have not been in. We will file your letter in our registry looking to that time in the future when they may come in expressing a similar desire and wanting to get in touch with you. Thank you for writing.*

*Sincerely,*
*Henry Bellmon*
*Director of Human Services.*

I was disappointed, but not surprised. I had told myself to expect disappointment so it didn't hurt as bad. On some level I knew this wasn't going to be easy. I had heard my entire life that adoptees "aren't allowed" to have information on who they are. This wasn't going to be a cakewalk.

My friend Denna heard about a woman named Irene who lived in Muskogee. This person, according to Denna, was a Native American "reader." Denna had worked in Muskogee, and knew all kinds of people from that area—old friends who had been co-workers—who had shared amazing tales with her about Irene's abilities to see the future.

We climbed into her yellow Toyota truck and took off to meet Irene for ourselves. The drive to Muskogee was quick. We arrived in a not-so-great neighborhood, and located a fairly impoverished-looking house surrounded by junk. There was stuff piled everywhere on everything, both inside and out.

A small, frail Native American lady greeted us. She didn't ask our names. In fact, she said, "Tell me nothing."

This diminutive woman ushered us into a very tiny room. We sat down, and she sat by me. She took a long, curious look at me. In a slow and methodical voice she said, "You will be like a woman I will read about in the paper, who has never met her biological parents, but will discover one day that she is a millionaire."

I thought, wow, how did this woman know that? How did she know I'm adopted? She continued by telling me that some of my relatives are Native American. "People will come into your life from a long way away," she said. "You've never met them but you will. The newspapers will want to talk to you but your family will want to keep you quiet." I was stunned. In fact, I don't know that I asked her another thing. Denna sat for her reading and we headed back to Tulsa.

I was watchful on the way home, because Irene had warned me to be careful—that men were going to follow me or perhaps come to my house. I remember Denna was even concerned about people following us home because that was such a weird thing to hear at a reading. We left with one eye looking over our shoulders, and comparing notes. Irene didn't have much detail, but what she had said was astounding, and echoed Lillie precisely.

In school I was matriculating nicely. I loved it, really. I knew that I was going to be a natural at therapy. I was working happily as a mental health technician—evenings at Shadow Mountain, and at St. John Hospital, another mental health facility, as well. I was so fortunate to have ended up at Shadow Mountain at this time, because they had started working with a man named Foster Cline, who was world-renowned for his work with attachment disordered kids. When I began my job at Shadow Mountain, I wanted to be the adoptee's therapist, and Foster Cline was offering training to be credentialed in attachment work. I was chomping at the bit to train with him. I got in. Foster Cline would personally train a group of us, and I would be credentialed, and could focus on precisely what had motivated me this far—precisely, in fact, what motivated a large part of my life. Working with him was amazing—one of the best professional experiences of my career.

After I was credentialed, I took over the Adoption Attachment Track at Shadow Mountain. It was my program. I really felt I had arrived.

My work became even more fulfilling. I really enjoyed doing hands-on work with adoptees and parents. They would tell me their stories and I would feel their emotions—deep down. I knew what that felt like. I had walked in the shoes of so many of them. I would often facilitate searches for them and help adoptive parents understand their children's need to connect to their origins.

I'm reminded of an interesting exercise I used with some of the kids. I'd ask them to draw a picture with their non-dominant hand (i.e. the one they did not ordinarily write with) of what they thought their birthmother looked like. It seemed there were always a few kids who drew famous people. One of the kids commented, "I've always wondered if my birth mom was a movie star."

I felt pity for such kids; how foolish to think their biological parents ever amounted to anything. I thought it would be equally foolish to assume the same about mine. Lillie had said all sorts of stuff about my biological parents—but nothing that seemed to add up to anything like "movie star." It was nice to think about but very unlikely. And Lillie had given a much different view of my biological father: alcoholism, black sheep, some abuse, family mysteries, and deceit…and the unambiguous message that neither my mother or my father wanted anything to do with me. That message I received clearly.

So I had compassion for the kids who wished for fame in their "real" families. Little could I have imagined my life experiences and shocking discoveries.

My fondness for animals intensified even more through these years at Shadow Mountain. I had always wanted a German shepherd. And back when I went to college, a friend had given me one I couldn't keep. I gave her to Mom and Dad, and they gave her to a man who owned a large farm so she could run and play. Sadly, she wandered from the place, and vanished.

But that little taste of German shepherd was enough to get me hooked, so I had to have another one. I was living in a house off Riverside Drive in Tulsa. After conducting a little canine research, I contacted the Schutzhund Club. It turned out there was a woman in the club who had a German female who had just had puppies—serendipity! But these pups were $500 each, which was a *lot* of money in the mid-eighties. Uncertain I could afford one, yet undeterred, I went over to see them. The pups were about six weeks old, and the cutest things I'd ever seen. One of the puppies came right over and put her little paw right on top of my hand—and just like that it was over.

I bought her.

She was the only black and tan pup of the whole litter. And it's funny how I actually got her. Schutzhund is basically a kind of suitability test that determines if a dog displays the appropriate traits and characteristics of certain lines of working dogs (although, today, many breeds other than German shepherd dogs compete)—especially for police-type work. Schutzhund tests for traits like courage, intelligence, trainability, and perseverance, as well as for physical traits such as strength, endurance, agility, and scenting ability.

The owner of the mother had made an agreement with the owner of the sire that in exchange for the stud fee he would get pick of the litter. One of the Schutzhund tests involves firing a pistol over the young pups to see which run in fear to hide, and which sit up and pay attention to what's going on. I was in the fenced-in area where the testing was being done, playing with her, and the trainer came by with that pistol, and fired it—kaBOOM! She bolted straight under my chair like a shot. It was the funniest and cutest thing to see. I was in love with that ball of fur. Thankfully, that shot marked the immediate end of her Schutzhund career—a failure which registered as a smashing success by placing her in my loving care. Her name was Kira and she began my history of many years of companionship with German dogs.

During my work with Foster Cline I met Pam Overhuls. Pam was head of Children's Services and was very involved with adoption and establishing "best practice" guidelines and legislation for the state. Pam belonged to some very important committees and organizations, and was an exceptional clinician. I was asked to serve on a legislative task force with her. She taught me a great deal about the "system" and advocated for more disclosure of information at the time of adoption. She was instrumental in making that happen, and adoptive parents were then able to more appropriately care for their kids, some of whom had very difficult beginnings with biological parents. Parents would no longer have to wonder about medical history, trauma, mental health issues, or the makeup of the biological family.

Pam was an inspiration to me. Tragically, she was killed in a freakish accidental fire on Christmas Eve. Her mom and sister left me the body of her work—the distillate of a lifetime of studying adoption and adoption-related legislation: boxes of research, valuable insights, and data. I would later assimilate much of her work into my own—speeches, therapy, activism, letter writing. Pam's was a legacy I wanted to honor with what I did.

I kept working to get more documents related to my own adoption. And I got a few, here and there, but the whole task was designed to be practically insurmountable.

Lillie never stopped telling me I'd had a "grandfather who loved me." That knowledge—that someone in my biological family had cared about me—pushed me with a vengeance to find him. I knew my mother didn't want me and my father didn't want me, but they would be the key to finding my granddad. I remember once even saying to Lillie that I didn't care much about finding my mom and dad—but would need to find them to get to him.

And how would my adoptive family take this? I wasn't sure. What I did know was I had to move forward. It was key to my happiness. I had a grandfather out there. He had loved me. I loved him right back. I felt certain my mom would be supportive, and I prayed she wouldn't feel as though she had failed me in any way. So often, I had listened to anguished adoptive parents lament that, if they had just been "better parents," their children wouldn't "need" to know their roots. I would help Mom understand that my need to know was in no way connected to any lack on her part. It was not about her. It was about what happened to me before her. I felt some anxiety and fear that I might hurt her; something I wanted to avoid but knew was a possibility.

My father was a very common-sense man. He seldom ventured out of his comfort zone and I doubted he would understand any of it. My biggest worry was Gran. She was horrified at the idea that I would want to know where I had come from, once telling my mom she didn't think it would be "a good idea." In fact, not long after I had arrived with my new family, Gran was approached with a proposition that I be the Gerber baby in ad campaigns. She was adamant that it not happen, as someone from my biological family might recognize me and "want you back." Discussion of my search was not to be shared with Gran.

Ultimately, I knew I would have to let go of the outcome and simply be as sensitive as I could to my family while not abandoning my own need to know. It was a rather lonely place to be.

"You will see papers…old and crumpling and yellow. They were written to you and will tell you the story. There will be tears and you won't believe that day. You love history. It's a shame they let you get away from them. Your grandfather was a part of history. There are papers. They'll tell you they didn't know where you were."

―――

*Lillie, 1990*

# 6

# "A catalogue of blunders"

The Thanksgiving holiday approached. It was 1985, and Aunt Jo was visiting from Colorado, where she'd lived since retiring from the Air Force.

I was working feverishly to track down my birth documentation, and had been told that even though I was born in Pottawattamie County, adoptions were always finalized where the adoptive parents lived. That meant there would be a trail of legal documents at the courthouse in Kay County, Oklahoma. I knew that the town of Newkirk was the county seat for Kay County.

I didn't have any specific plan of "attack" in mind. I thought I would just show up at the Kay County courthouse and start asking some questions, and hope to find a kind soul who might find it in his heart to help me. Law and order had robbed me of my identity, perhaps a little mercy and kindness would help keep me on the trail.

I convinced Mom and Aunt Jo to join me on the thirty-mile trip to Newkirk. With no more documentation in my possession than my adoption decree, we drove to the courthouse, trundled up the marble steps and through the beveled glass doors, and entered the clerk's office.

The place was a busy, buzzing hub of action. Several women behind the counter kept paper moving and phones from clattering. One of the clerks approached and I placed my decree on the counter, saying, "Hi, I'm wondering if you can give me some information about this case."

She took the decree, and said, "Well, I guess if the judge gave you the order, I can give you the information."

I was shocked that she said the word "order," but assumed she just misspoke.

She took the decree with her and vanished into the myriad of offices behind. Time passed. Seven or eight minutes seemed to drag into hours. She returned and handed me some documents.

I was flabbergasted when I glanced at them and realized what they were. I was holding the complete record of my adoption case. Mom and Jo realized, too, that a mistake had been made in our favor. My eyes scanned the pages frantically, searching for names, names, names—skimming them as fast as possible before the clerk caught her mistake and snatched the documents from me.

Once I'd read all I could, cramming as much as possible into my short-term memory, I mustered the courage to ask, "Can you make me a copy of this?" Then I panicked, thinking I might have just called attention to the mistake and blown it all; but at least I had the names in my head.

"Sure," the clerk replied, "but it will cost a dollar a page."

Those would be the happiest dollars I had ever spent. She actually copied the documents and gave them to me. At this point I realized she wouldn't notice her mistake—that she had confused an adoption decree for an order for adoption records. She probably handled so many orders every day that she went on a sort of autopilot. Or perhaps mercy and kindness sometimes manifest karmically, in the carelessness of your nemesis.

Mom understood precisely what had happened too, and she was in no mood to linger at the scene. "Come on, let's get outta here, we're going have the police after us!" she said.

Aunt Jo kept saying, "What is it? What's the problem?"

We casually but quickly scooted out of there with the

goods in hand. Arriving home, we were free to study them carefully. All the same names appeared in the new documents, so I presumed they were correctly filed, and that Robert Gafford and Irene Pruitt, the names on my birth certificate, must be correct—though the certificate spelled the name "Gaffard."

Naturally, I launched a national search for Irene Pruitt. This was before the Internet, so I didn't have the benefit of search tools like Ancestry.com. But during my work with adoptees, I had met a lot of nationally known adoption experts.

Among them was a woman called a "search angel." This is a term given to people who conduct searches at no cost for adoptees. She had tremendous access to records—including court documents, government records, libraries, and Social Security databases—and had located over 3,000 birthparents. In her entire career there were only two people whose birthparents she hadn't found.

Guess who would be the third.

She uncovered nothing on Irene Pruitt—as if the woman didn't exist.

I decided to keep searching. If I couldn't find my birthmother, I would track down every single name that appeared anywhere on any shred of documentation at all related to my entire life or history. Exhaustive enough for you? Well, I was even more thorough than that: I decided to find every person ever associated in any way with the events surrounding my birth.

The name Polly Hunt appeared as a caseworker, so I looked through the Oklahoma City phonebook. I found a Polly Hunt listed, so I dialed the number and waited for someone to pick up.

When she answered, I heard birds chirping in the background. Apparently she had a parrot.

I told Polly Hunt my story, and what I was looking for. She said she had indeed worked in adoptions for the Department of Human Services and would try to help me if I would call back the very next day. That request seemed a bit odd to me, but I was excited to have found the right person. This was a break in the case. The very woman whose name appeared on my documents was reasonably friendly and accommodating, and seemed willing to help me out.

I stayed up late, laying out all my questions and anticipating the next day with eager excitement. I woke up early, had breakfast, ticked off the hours, and then called her. And she said the strangest thing:

"You know, I hadn't seen Bonnie Walton in over thirty years, but I just saw her at a funeral yesterday, and she reminded me I can't talk about any of this stuff—these old cases, and whatnot."

Click.

And just like that, she severed ties.

Surely there was no way in the universe that Polly Hunt happened to run into Bonnie Walton at a funeral—one day after I had requested her help with my own case history and story.

Bonnie Walton was the corporealization of "The System." She embodied every ugly, unjust, and immoral measure the state had ever taken against me. But I knew she might be the only connection to a potential break in the case. So I remained quite cordial. I wondered, many times, if she understood what the information she guarded meant to individuals seeking their own personal truths; whether she had any awareness of the sadness and grief the system perpetuated in those they professed to "protect."

As time passed and I relocated, I always let the department know where I was. In 1987 I reached out to Bonnie Walton with one such update:

*Dear Ms. Walton:*

*Some time ago I wrote regarding my natural mother (copy enclosed). I would like to provide you with my new address and phone number in the event*

*an inquiry occurs. Thank you for your time.*
*Sincerely,*
*Rhonda Noonan*

A few months later, I had another Lillie reading. She told me that I had four half-sisters on my mother's side. And she talked more about my grandfather: "You know, if you opened a history book, there he would be."

I thought it was silly at the time. But so many other things she said were right, that I kept paying close attention. She talked about my biological father and his relationship with his dad—how he had a terrible temper, constantly fighting with him.

She asked me early on if I was aware that my biological father had known about me. She said he knew very well he had a daughter, and had even told some of his family members about it. She said I would meet some of those family members someday, and come to know a few of them very well.

She encouraged me to keep looking and not give up. "You will find him...that I can tell you. It is supposed to be that way." I can assure you, I had my doubts.

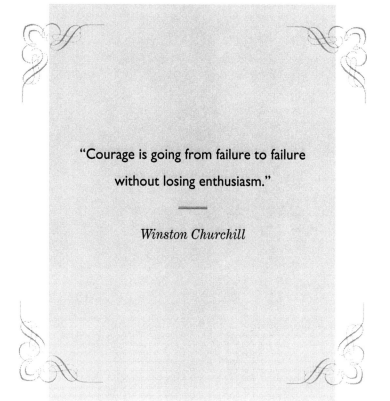

"Courage is going from failure to failure without losing enthusiasm."

_Winston Churchill_

# 7

# "A bodyguard of lies"

S everal years passed, throughout which I kept searching—relentlessly. My persistence paid off late in 1989, when I got a response from Child Welfare Services.

*Dear Ms. Noonan:*

*We have received your letter requesting all pertinent case information regarding medical and/or background from your adoption file. The attached confidential material from our microfilm files is all the information we have on file relating to these areas. We can only provide one copy due to staff and cost constraints. Please feel free to make copies to share with any professionals involved in this case. We are hopeful that this material will be helpful to you. We are unable to release any names as this information is confidential by law.*

*Sincerely,*

*James Bohanon*

*Supervisor*

*Child Welfare Services.*

*NOTE: We have double-checked our registry and no one from your birth family has contacted us seeking a reunion. We will notify you should they do so in the future.*

*Circumstances leading to child's removal from home:*

*Mother's 4 children unaware of this pregnancy, and mother went to great lengths to keep this pregnancy from them. Mother voluntarily relinquished rights before judge. She felt unable to afford to raise a 5th child on her already inadequate income.*

*Siblings and Birthdates:*
*½ sister Zelpha 1942–9th grade, dark brown hair and eyes–quiet and reserved–attractive.*
*½ sister Lenore 1943–8th grade, seemed advanced–outgoing.*
*½ sister Lynda 1944–6th grade, quiet, reserved, makes good grades.*
*½ sister Caroline 1947 – outgoing, happy.*

*MOTHER OF CHILD FOR ADOPTIVE PLACEMENT:*
*Birthdate: 1922*
*Widow*
*Race: white*
*Nationality: Irish and Black Dutch*
*Physical Description: 5'4.5", 130 pounds (square face), brown eyes, light brown hair (very attractive appearance).*
*Religion: Baptist*
*Personality: Nice, co-operative.*
*Education level: HS graduate & Beauty college*
*Work record: Sales, beautician*
*Diseases/Illnesses: Good health.*
*Handicaps: None.*
*No complications during any of the pregnancies.*
*Grandmother's age: 68*
*Race: W*
*Grandparents occupation: Farmers*
*Both died of strokes.*

*[ALLEGED] FATHER OF CHILD FOR ADOPTIVE*
*PLACEMENT:*
*Birthdate: Age 30-37*
*Status: Unknown*
*Phsyical Description: 5'11", 180, nice looking, brown*
*hair, brown eyes.*
*Work record: Government employee*

"Alleged" was written in by hand.

This was the biggest break in the case so far. Mr. Bohannon was so helpful, that I wrote back to ask him to check on my time of birth. He responded in November:

> *Dear Ms. Noonan:*
>   *At your request, the adoption record was checked*
> *again, but there is no entry for your time of birth. It is*
> *with regret that we report that we are unable to assist you.*
>                    *Sincerely,*
>                    *James Bohanon*
>                    *Supervisor*
>                    *Child Welfare Services*

I could only sigh. As ever, the search was proving to be a roller-coaster. There had been so many years of fruitless activities punctuated by so many intermittent leads—after which I always seemed to be knocked back to square one.

November blustered in, and it started turning chilly. I visited Lillie for some powerful readings. Here is my transcript of what she told me:

> *There are relatives or friends coming to see you.*
> *I believe you'll meet your birthmother.*
> *You may be Indian.*

*I see the state of Missouri.*
*Your birthmother was alone when you were born.*
*Her husband was dead or not there.*
*Your birthfather knew about you. You will get an inheritance.*
*Your biological mother may be sick.*
*Your mother may be dark-haired and brown-eyed.*
*Someone loves you and their name starts with a "C".*
*A dark man with broad shoulders will visit you.*
*Really good things will happen.*
*There may be a brother coming to talk face to face.*
*You'll take a trip in the future to a distant place.*
*Your whole family will be in the newspaper.*
*An article in the newspaper will be the opening for all this to transpire.*
*Your grandfather never got over you being given away. He was mad as thunder.*
*There are not many left in your biological family; lots of deaths.*
*I am anxious for you to get your grandpa's picture.*
*You'll meet people who knew him.*
*A man is going to bring you a message. A man from the same family. He thinks it has gone on long enough. He will bring the message to you.*
*You will get a cedar chest, and albums. One young fella your age will be footloose and fancy-free and will show you around.*
*Your grandfather wrote things down to explain to you.*
*There are trunks crammed full of stuff that no one's looked at that belong to you.*
*You will go a lot of places like England.*

Autumn gave way to winter, and in the bitter cold of February came the best news yet. I was working at Shadow Mountain and was searching for one of my kid's biological parents. I became aware of a special district judge out of Oklahoma County who would give court orders for the release of birth certificates to adoptees.

I quickly wrote to this judge and told him I was a mental health therapist, and was myself adopted, and wanted his help. Much to my joyful shock I received this:

*Dear Rhonda Jean Noonan,*

*Enclosed is the order to release to you, your original Birth Certificate. You must tender this order to the bureau of Vital Statistics yourself.*

*Sincerely,*

*Judge Charles Kelley*

I was ecstatic. Finally, I got what anyone else in America can have in one trip to the Department of Vital Statistics! What takes the average citizen two hours to acquire, had taken me more than twenty years. I hoped it would provide the all-important information I needed.

I sent my court order straight away:

*Mr. Roger C. Pirrong,*
*State Registrar, Vital Record*

*Dear Mr. Pirrong*

*Enclosed you will find the following: a copy of my current birth certificate, a copy of the letter from Judge Charles Kelley concerning this matter, and the original order to have my birth certificate released to me. Please forward my original birth certificate to me at my current address.*

*Thank you very much for your assistance.*

*Sincerely,*

*Rhonda Noonan*

A week passed. I waited on pins and needles, racing home each day to check the mail. And finally I received it:

*CERTIFICATE OF LIVE BIRTH*
*State of Oklahoma Department of Health.*
*ISSUED IN ACCORDANCE WITH COURT – BY*
    *JUDGE: CHARLES KELLEY, DISTRICT OF*
    *OKLAHOMA COUNTY, 8 DAY OF MARCH 1990.*
*CHILD'S NAME: Rene Irene Gaffard,*
*FATHER'S NAME: Robert Gaffard*
*MOTHER'S MAIDEN NAME: Irene Pruitt.*
*Shawnee City Hospital, 1115 No. Broadway, Shawnee,*
    *Oklahoma*
*July 8, 1956*

This was a huge deal. I had waited all my life for this piece of paper. And now I had two names…on my original birth certificate!

Three months passed, and I found my myself at another dead end. I'd tried tracking down every piece of information I received in September. It was alleged that my birthmother worked as a beautician, which is not easy to do without a license. And if one were practicing without a license, one would hardly admit it on a government document. I was determined to find my mom's cosmetology license—as confirmation that there was a shred of truth in her story. I received word on it in June of the next year:

*Dear Ms. Noonan,*

    *We have researched our records for an Irene Pruitt and an Irene Gafford and can find no record of a cosmetologist licensed or having been licensed under these two names. Perhaps the person in ques-*

*tion has changed her name. Perhaps this person is*
*a barber? The barber advisory board may be able to*
*further assist you in this matter.*

*Sincerely,*
*Jennifer McRee*
*Oklahoma State Board of*
*Cosmetology*

I drove to Shawnee to try to find the hospital I was born in. I took a friend with me; we researched high-school yearbooks and scoured the town, talking to people in the area about my birth address.

We found the hospital, but they had destroyed all records over ten years old when the old edifice was torn down to build the new one. However, we found the doctor who delivered me. We actually phoned him and spoke to him. Unfortunately he didn't remember anything about anyone from 1956.

I came away from the Shawnee visit convinced that my birthmother never lived there, but had just moved there to have me.

Toward the end of 1990, I started making what felt like a little bit of progress. In September, my attorney asked the court for an order:

*The Honorable Judge Charles Kelley*

*Dear Judge Kelley:*
*I represent Rhonda Jean Noonan, an adopted child,*
*in her search for her birthmother and natural father.*
*Ms. Noonan is contemplating conceiving a child, and at*
*the age of 34 is legitimately concerned about any genetic*
*abnormalities that she may pass on to an unborn child.*
*Ms. Noonan is seeking an order to release all*
*adoption records not already obtained by her. Pre-*

*viously, she has obtained some court files from both Pottawatomie and Kay counties (where the adoption proceedings were held) and some non-identifying information from the Department of Human Services (DHS). Also, earlier this year, you issued an order to release her original birth certificate. Copies of these documents are enclosed.*

*These documents, however, are disturbingly inconsistent, and are hampering Ms. Noonan's search. Pursuant to the authority granted to the court by Title 10 O.S. Secs. 60.17 and 60.18, I have enclosed an Order that would release the complete adoption file from DHS (previously the Department of Public Welfare). I have also enclosed a letter from a doctor stating that releasing the information is in the best interest of Ms. Noonan.*

*While we would prefer an order releasing all information, Ms. Noonan feels it most critical at this time that she obtain the complete birthplace and complete birthdate of her birthmother, both of which are conspicuously absent from any of the documentation already obtained by Ms. Noonan.*

*Judge Kelley, we feel the inconsistencies necessitate the release, and can only be cleared up by an examination of all adoption records. While we are not alleging that a fraud was perpetrated on the Court in 1956 and 1957, we think the circumstances definitely warrant the release of all information. Here are just a few of the inconsistencies we have found:*

*1. Baby Girl Gafford/Gaffard was born on July 8, 1956, and on the Petition, Waiver of Appearance, and Order dated July 16, and July 17, 1956, respectively, she is listed as the "illegitimate child of Irene Pruitt and Robert Gafford." On the Petition for Adoption and*

*Decree of Adoption dated March 27, 1957, the mother is shown as Irene Gafford. On the original birth certificate, the name of the mother is listed as Irene Pruitt, which is indicated as the mother's "Maiden Name." The inconsistency in names is puzzling. We suppose the confusion could result from either a formal or common law marriage to Robert Gafford. But, DHS records from 1956 list the mother as "Widow" even though the March, 1957 documents indicate a shared residence between Irene Pruitt and Robert Gafford.*

*2. Although it is evident that Irene Gafford had a sustained relationship with Robert Gafford, and listed him as the father of the child on the birth certificate, she supplied DHS with the following information concerning him: marital status of father "unknown"; father's identity "alleged"; age unknown ("30-37"); government employee; race, nationality unknown. This information is inconsistent with information on the birth certificate, which lists Robert Gafford, a "white male" as the father, working at "International Building."*

*3. No address is given for the mother or father in any court document in our possession, with the statement that the mother has "no home of her own." On the birth certificate, however, a residence, "1115 No. Broadway, Shawnee, OK", is given.*

*We feel time is of the essence in this matter. As I indicated, the Order and the supporting documentation is enclosed. We appreciate your assistance in this matter.*

*Sincerely,*
*Kellie J. Watts*

If he gave me the birth certificate, I reasoned, he might be sympathetic to adopted adults, so we'd try to get my whole file. The very next day the Judge issued the Order:

*FILED–DISTRICT COURT OKLAHOMA COUN-TY, TOM PETUSKEY COURT CLERK: in the Matter of the Adoption of BABY GIRL GAFFORD, Case #1676–APPLICATION AND ORDER TO RE-LEASE ALL ADOPTION RECORDS FROM DE-PARTMENT OF HUMAN SERVICES:*

*COMES NOW, the Applicant and states to the Court that the applicant is an adopted child and said child was born on the 8th of July in 1956, in the State of Oklahoma. That pursuant to the authority granted to the Court, Applicant hereby requests that all adop-tion records held by the Department of Human Ser-vices to be released to applicant.*

*NOW ON THIS 5th DAY of September, 1990, the Court has considered the above application, and is fully advised in the premises.*

*THEREFORE IT IS HEREBY ORDERED AND DECREED that the Department of Human Services (DHS) is Ordered to release to applicant all adoption records held by DHS concerning BABY GIRL GAFFORD/GAFFARD, born on the 8th day of July, 1956.*

*JUDGE CHARLES KELLEY.*

Surely this was too good to be true. Judge Charles Kelley has *ordered* DHS to release my entire adoption file, which means they had to, because a Judge had legal power to compel them. Yay!

I scheduled the earliest time available, then drove to Oklahoma City with my attorney, Kellie Watts, and a friend, Lenya Robinson. Lenya was an amateur sleuth of sorts, and had helped me with a great deal of research. We entered the Sequoyah Building and informed the attendant we'd like to see Bonnie Walton.

"I have a court order to release my complete adoption file." The words tasted so good in my mouth.

I was surprised that Bonnie came straight out to talk to me, and said that what I was asking for was "against the law." She went on to explain that in the entire time she had been head of that department, she had only seen one other court order for the release of records—because it's against the law, and didn't we know that? And besides, it needed "to come from the county you were adopted in, not this one," she stated, triumphantly.

They escorted Kellie, Lenya and me to a conference room off the lobby, and suggested we have a seat and wait; they would get back to us. It was probably forty-five minutes before they returned. They said they had discussed the issue with the judge and he had rescinded the order. Bonnie came out with the attorneys, and sat on one side of the table, and Kellie, Lenya, and I sat on the other.

"What do you want to stop this whole thing?" Bonnie asked. "You know that very few people know who your biological father was. His name is nowhere in the records. In the whole file there is only one place in which there is a clue as to his identity." She paused, and then asked again, "What do you want to know to stop this?"

"I want my mother's date of birth, and I want to know if the people on my birth certificate are my biological parents."

"Yes," Bonnie answered.

At that moment I saw one of the attorneys look directly at her and give her an astonished look of admonishment. At one point all three of them left the room to confer, and Lenya later confessed that it was all she could do to keep herself from grabbing the file right off the table and darting out of the building. I shared that thought. But there were security guards everywhere—we never would've made it out. The attorneys came back in and I stated, quite matter-of-factly, "I understand my father was someone important."

"We wouldn't know about that," replied one of the attorneys.

"If you don't, who does, then?" I said, pressing the issue. "You win today, but I can assure you this is not the end of this. I will never stop."

"That's all?" asked Bonnie Walton.

"One other thing, my biological mom's birth date."

She gave me a date, and we departed the building.

After that trip to Oklahoma City, lines were clearly drawn. There were friends and there were enemies, and DHS fell firmly into latter camp. It was clear that the people there and the system they were controlling would work as hard as they could to hide, confuse, and hamper any and all efforts I made to find out what everyone else I knew had a legal right to from the second they were born. DHS was corrupt. I suspected I had been lied to and I was tired of it. Mindless bureaucracy...that was the name of this game. When I watched them scoff in the face of a court order from a Judge, I got the first profound realization of just what kind of second-class citizens adoptees really are.

I phoned Peg Davidson, the searcher in Houston, and told her, "I have a name *and* a birthdate." She said she would get right on it.

About three days later she called and said she wasn't having any luck with the date. She called back a week later and said, "I've searched everywhere...there's less than a one in three million chance that anyone with this name was born on this date." Then she said, "I can tell you with a fair amount of certainty that there is no such person."

At this point I began wondering, was this woman I was searching for ever a real person? I headed back to Tulsa, and as soon as I walked in the front door I heard the phone ringing.

It was Bonnie Walton calling. She said, "I just wanted you to know that I made a mistake. The man listed on your birth certificate died three years before you were born."

"I know," I told her.

I had already been told by Lillie that the man whose name was on my birth certificate was not my real father. I wasn't the least bit surprised that I had been lied to. The "department" would feed me any line of nonsense to try to keep me in the dark.

I resented all that Bonnie Walton represented. However, in less than a year, she would be gone. Her long career at DHS would end, and she would be replaced by another director.

On September 12 we asked the Kay County judge to compel DHS to comply with the Order issued by Judge Kelley.

*September 12, 1990*
*The Honorable Judge Neal Beekman*
*District Court Kay County, Oklahoma*

*Dear Judge Beekman:*

*I represent Rhonda Jean Noonan, an adopted child, in her search for her birthmother and natural father. Ms. Noonan is contemplating conceiving a child, and at the age of 34, is legitimately concerned about any genetic abnormalities that she may pass on to an unborn child.*

*Ms. Noonan is seeking an order to release all adoption records not already obtained by her. Previously, she has obtained some court files from both Pottawatomie and Kay counties (where the adoption proceedings were held) and some non-identifying information from the department of human services (DHS). Also, earlier this year, you issued an order to release her original birth certificate. Copies of these documents are enclosed.*

*Perhaps most importantly, however, just last week,*

*Judge Charles Kelley, and Oklahoma County Special Judge, ordered DHS to release Ms. Noonan's entire adoption file based on a showing of "good cause." DHS refuses to comply with this Order based upon jurisdictional issues, [which I dispute based on a strict reading of Title 10 O.S. 60.17(C)], and plans to file a Motion to Vacate the Order. But, they have informed me that they would honor an Order from Kay County to release the files. While the challenge to the Oklahoma County order is pending, I am seeking an order from your court pursuant to Title 10 O.S. Secs. 60.17 and 60.18, to compel DHS to release my client's adoption files. For your review, I have enclosed all the supporting documentation provided to Judge Kelley from which he made his decision.*

*For your information, we pursued an Oklahoma County District Court Order because Oklahoma County is the county in which DHS sits and in which the files are physically located. Also, earlier this year, Judge Kelley issued an order to release my client's original birth certificate.*

*We also have been made aware of the fact that my client's biological mother, Irene Pruitt-Gafford, was a personal friend of her DHS adoption unit worker, who may have assisted Ms. Pruitt-Gafford in laying down a fraudulent information trail. We feel time is of the essence in this matter. As I indicated, the Order and the supporting documentation are enclosed. We appreciate your assistance in this matter.*

*Sincerely,*
*Kellie J. Watts*

Judge Beekman did not grant the request, and I hired Camille Quinn to sue DHS:

*October 7, 1991*
*Ms. Jane Morgan*
*Program Supervisor*
*Division of Child Welfare*

*Dear Ms. Morgan:*

*Since my attempts at reaching you by phone have failed, I am writing this letter to advise you of recent action taken by Ms. Rhonda Noonan. I have been retained by Ms. Noonan to cause her adoption file to be judicially opened. Please be aware that Ms. Noonan is ready to proceed against DHS in District Court for Kay County, in the State of Oklahoma. Ms. Noonan is prepared to present evidence that DHS has voluntarily and willingly assisted in searches on behalf of adopted persons seeking a reunion with biological parents, while DHS refuses to help her do the same. It is well founded that an organization which operates at public expense is prohibited from selectively enforcing its policies. Ms. Noonan's sole goal is for her biological family to be contacted by an objective, neutral third party who would inform the family of Ms. Noonan's whereabouts and inform them that she seeks a reunion. Since DHS has willingly provided this service to many Oklahomans whose situations were similar to Ms. Noonan's, it is curious that DHS declines assistance to only Rhonda Noonan. If you will consent to a proposal regarding the use of a third party to assist Ms. Noonan, then she will drop any present or future cause of action to have her adoption records opened against DHS, or any of the DHS staff in either their personal or agency capacity. The offer outlined in this letter will remain open until November 1, 1991 at 5:00 p.m.*

*Sincerely,*
*Camille Quinn*

They called the bluff. They sent nothing. I couldn't afford to sue them. Or rather, I could afford to initiate a suit, but the reality was I would get nowhere with it. I knew that records were released to some adopted persons. I had clients whose adoptive parents had managed to secure information from DHS that identified biological parents. The double standards and the "it's all in who you know" culture was infuriating to me. I continued...forward.

Since I was originally told, by my adoptive family, that my biological father was killed in a car wreck, I began searching records for high profile politicians who died in auto accidents within nine months of my birth. There was no one.

I had always contemplated hiring a private investigator, but they were expensive, and I was a pretty decent sleuth myself, so I never justified the expense. But now, out of leads and out of ideas, I broke down and hired an investigator.

*October 23, 1992*
*I, Rhonda Noonan, do hereby engage and autho-*
*rize G.M. Investigations to conduct a private investiga-*
*tion on my behalf and to submit to me a written report.*

"You have enemies? Good. That means you've stood up for something sometime in your life."

———

*Winston Churchill*

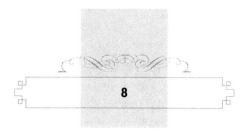

**8**

# "The courage to continue"

After a month of hard work, the investigator had found nothing. Private investigators are expensive, and a month goes by quickly. I couldn't afford to re-hire him, so I resumed my own self-styled sleuthing, which to that point had yielded more than any external help.

I longed for distractions from work and searching. A co-worker, Taylor Burns, was taking a recreational therapy exam in Kansas City. I decided to go along for the ride and get away for the weekend. On the drive up, I heard on the car radio that there was a horse-and-tack sale at the stockyards the following day. I had Taylor drop me off there so I could check out the sale while he went and sat for his exam.

I wandered through all the vendors and the people, and soon I came upon the saddles. I had always loved the the smells of farms, fairs, and rodeos—the distinct aroma of live-stock. And ever since I was a small child obsessed with hors-es, I had wanted a saddle. The saddle makers around Kansas City produced some remarkable examples. The craftsman-ship was excellent. I browsed and browsed, finally narrowing down to my favorite one—and then I bought my first saddle.

Naturally, it doesn't make much sense to have a saddle if you don't have anything to put it on. I thought perhaps if I just got the saddle to start, it would motivate me to get a truck, and a place in the country, and— eventually—I would purchase a horse to go with it all. As if to provide extra motivation, I didn't stop at the saddle…not with aisles and aisles of vendors displaying their best wares. There was more stuff than you could ever really look at in a day. I saw so many irresistible items that by the time Taylor came back after his exam, I had added a pile of acquisitions to my new saddle: spurs, buckets, brushes, halters and leads, a bridle, everything.

Taylor said, "What on earth are you doing, Rhonda?!"

"Making sure that someday I'm gonna have to have a horse."

He rolled his eyes, but he was a good friend, and good friends know the importance of indulging each other's dreams.

Shortly thereafter the auction exploded into action, with people bidding like mad on the horses. Hands were flying up and livestock was selling fast. Another one, and another one, and another one.

"Hititadimehititamore, going once!…going twice!…Three times…Sold!

A seemingly endless parade of horses were being auctioned off. I was mesmerized. A little yearling paint hit the block, the bidding started, and the next thing I saw was Taylor's arm going up, and then again and again, until—"Sold!"—he'd bought that yearling paint colt for three hundred and fifty bucks.

He looked at me and said, "You have to help yourself, and if your dream is to have a horse, then just step up and buy one. We're not leaving here till you buy a horse."

Simple logistics seemed to preclude my having a horse anytime soon. I drove a small sports car and lived in the city. How and where in the world was I going to keep it? And yet I went outside and started looking through the animals for sale.

My gaze fixed on a quarter-horse mare. I was smitten. I followed her, watching as she promptly entered the auction and was sold for way more money than I could ever have afforded. *Wow, horses can get expensive*, I thought. I was a little disappointed that someone else had bought her, and started to consider that maybe this wasn't supposed to happen at this point in my life.

Then along came Bubba. His full name was "Boones Shine Guy," and he was a toe-tapping, dancing, handsome little dude; a small black-and-white cow horse. He could turn on a dime, and was just one of the most beautiful and lovable horses I'd ever seen. I bought him.

I paid $1,450, and found a rancher who would let him stay at their farm in Kansas until I could make arrangements for him and pick him up. They were so helpful that they even arranged to have shoes put on him.

When I got home I borrowed my dad's truck, rented a horse trailer, drove back to Kansas, collected my first horse, and wept tears of joy all the way from Kansas City back to Tulsa.

Bubba was a double-registered paint and pinto. He was the grandson of a very successful Oklahoma race horse, and I was absolutely joyous. I found some pasture to lease at 91st and Mingo in Tulsa, and moved him there.

I continued to see Lillie. She expanded on the core story I had been told about my family. The more time that went by, the greater detail she was able to see. She had become a sweet friend and a source of encouragement and support for me.

I learned more about her past. She began seeing the future when she was three years old. Her uncle was going off to World War I and she had visions in which she saw him being killed; she knew he would never come home. Lillie's mother was filled with anger about her "gift," and instructed her to stop telling what she saw. She beat her if she caught Lillie talking to others about the future and said she was "of the Devil."

It wasn't long until the folks in her hometown caught wind of her mystical powers. The townspeople would sneak through their yard under the cover of darkness and knock on young Lillie's bedroom window to ask her questions. She would try to help them, but if her mother overheard anything she would be in serious trouble.

I never asked about her transition to reading palms, but once she said, "When you open your hands, the story of your life is there...and anybody who can read palms can tell it to you." She stared at my hand, then went on: " Some people have just a few lines, and some people have some really complex lines. You have the most interesting hands I've seen. I could look at your hands all day." Sometimes she would say, "Put your hands up," and she would press hers against mine—palm to palm.

One day I knocked on her back door (from where I could hear a western movie playing at full gallop). As she let me in I saw that it was a John Wayne movie. She said, "You know, I met him. He used to come here for readings."

"No way!" I said.

"Yes, John Wayne and Ben Johnson used to come here for readings from time to time...they were really nice people."

I often took people to see her—many of them doubters—and they would lie to her, trying to test her. I once took a friend of mine who was pregnant. She decided to tell Lillie that she was only two months pregnant, not six. When she came out of the reading room her eyes were as big as paper plates. She said she told Lillie how long she had been pregnant, and Lillie shook her head.

"No." Lillie said. "You are going to have this baby on December twelfth, and it will be a boy." This date was two days after her actual due date. The baby (a boy) was born exactly when Lillie said.

Lillie was a deeply spiritual woman. She was God-fearing, precious, and indescribably kind. I was saddened by the way she had been persecuted by the Christian brethren of her hometown. They accused her of being "of the devil," just as her mother had claimed. Yet twice a month, she had food taken to elderly people who couldn't afford it. She went to the grade school and, after inquiring as to need, would pay for the children's lunches if their family couldn't. The epitaph chiseled into her tombstone really sums up her journey in this world: She spent her life helping others.

As I got closer to Lillie, I used to take her out to eat. We had fried chicken at Judy Anne's. As we ate she would talk about her nephew who raised Appaloosas and lived in Pawhuska. She said one day I would have Appaloosas. She described all the houses I would ever live in. She used to tell me a lot about the animals I would have, too.

I lived in a town called Sapulpa, in a great house with a yard that sloped into a creek, backed by a huge hill. You couldn't ride a horse on the hill, because it was covered in bushes—tremendous underbrush that you would never want to try to navigate. It was a habit of mine to let Bubba wander out of his paddock, and he would sometimes go next door and hang out with the neighbor horse. I put a chain across the driveway so he would have the run of the place. One day, Bubba decided he would just head on out, up that hill. I heard a frantic whinny. Sure enough, he had gone straight up and couldn't figure out how to get back down. He began to panic, and started racing back and forth along the top, hollering for help.

I rescued him, and all was well. He had learned a good lesson. The next time I saw Lillie she was laughing so hard she could barely speak "That horse of yours will never go up that hill again!" she said. "He got up there once and couldn't get down." It was amazing how she could see even the most inconsequential moments of my everyday life.

There were many days when I felt totally without resources or ideas with regard to my search. I knew that the facts had been carefully covered up and time continued to pass. I didn't know which direction to go. Each time I had an idea of where or what to research, I followed it.

I sometimes would call Lillie and ask for a reading. Then I would hear the story one more time. The repeated parts were not very exciting, but I would wait with bated breath for new details that recontextualized the older readings. It was always exciting and uplifting on balance.

There were many, many things she accurately told me that came to pass. She always knew what houses I would buy. She knew all about my house in Colorado; it was white with a long driveway—a quarter mile, in fact. Lillie told me that it was "on the water." Well, I knew there was no water nearby, but I didn't say anything. I soon learned that my new house was sitting on an aquifer. Lillie said it's "like you're sitting on a whole lake." And she was literally right.

In what I thought might mean a solid break in the case, I learned that the State of Oklahoma had plans to use intermediaries to help adoptees find their birthparents—for a fee. They would then notify them of your desire to connect, and they could agree or not. If the parents said no, they could only legally be contacted one more time. So I knew if we found my birthparents we would have two shots at getting them to meet me.

I would start with my birthmother. I signed up immediately, submitted all the documents, and waited, and hoped, and prayed.

Bingo.

In 1998, the intermediary program found her; but she said she wouldn't meet me. Most people never got to talk to their own intermediaries, but I got to talk to mine. So I learned what my birthmother had told her.

"I have expected a call like this every day of my life," she had said. "I don't want any contact with her, none of my daughters knows about her, and I want to keep it that way."

The intermediary explained to me, "Okay, I have only one more try at this. So what, if anything, do you want me to ask her when I talk to her?"

"What were the circumstances surrounding my birth?" I answered. "And who was my dad?"

When she spoke with her for the final time, my mother explained that being a single parent with four kids, she couldn't afford another child. She said my father was someone she hadn't known. After the intermediary ended the second conversation, she phoned me back with the disheartening news: "Your birthmother is not going to budge."

It was right around this time that I lost my Kira.

Lillie was mainly a cat person, but she loved Kira too. She had told me once that Kira had dysplasia and two years later, she was diagnosed with it. When she was twelve years old, the dysplasia began to affect her life. Lillie would tell me how embarrassed the dog was. She couldn't go outside and couldn't get up and down on her own. It was a disgusting and agonizing sight to behold.

"I can tell you, unless you have her put to sleep, she'll hang on a long time. She thinks she needs to take care of you," Lillie explained.

I wasn't getting any rest from tending to Kira through the night. I went to see my doctor, as I wasn't feeling well. I hadn't had two straight hours of sleep in a week.

He said, "I can tell you, it's you or the dog."

I knew he was right. And Kira was so humiliated by her condition that it was crueler to keep her in this world than to see her out of it. But, God, what an unholy nightmare—putting a pet to sleep. I can't even believe I phrased it that way—Kira wasn't just *going to sleep*.

What a gruesome and agonizing position to be in. I knew I had to take her in, and I knew the longer I waited the worse it would get, and the crueler it was to her in the end. So I took her.

That was the hardest thing I'd ever done.

The vet gave her the shot to relax her. Then he said he would give her a hefty dose of the chemicals. It was totally surreal—like a scene from a movie...and a horror movie, at that. But it wasn't a movie, and we weren't actors. This was real.

The chemicals were supposed to start acting fast, but she didn't go out for a while. So the vet gave her another dose... and then a third.

Three shots, count 'em: one, two, three—all in the abdomen. Finally, she succumbed. I felt like vomiting and screaming at the same time. It was as out-of-body as an experience can get, and I thought I would have a nervous breakdown. I imagined that must be what one feels like.

I miss her still.

When I went back to see Lillie after that nightmare, she just said, "I'm so sorry...Kira did not want to leave you."

"It was sheer hell," I said.

The outpouring of sympathy from my friends was comforting. Several of them sent flower arrangements to my house.

It's not unusual for people who have suffered severe early loss to attach to animals, because animals are safe. They don't leave you. They love you unconditionally. The fear of abandonment is removed from the equation. All in all I've had three shepherds in my life, but never another Kira.

Life continued at its normal pace. I was working for a new company and searching for clues to my identity. Ever since I was young, I had wanted to live in Colorado, and my new company offered me a chance to direct their operations there.

A change sounded good. I needed some kind of forward movement in my life. I was in a quandary about my own history, and how to proceed with searching. I still didn't even know if the names on my own birth certificate were real. Can you even imagine that? How was I supposed to find anyone when I didn't even know who I was looking for?

I loaded up all my stuff in Oklahoma and moved to Colorado, but not before making a weekend trip in advance. I went out to get the lay of the land, and to look for houses. I found a perfect house near Westcliffe, and bought it. It was breathtaking—thirty-five acres with mountain views on two sides. The two years I would spend there were two of the happiest of my life. It was such an adventure. I made some wonderful friends and soon told people about my adoption case and its tribulations. Different people would occasionally offer advice or make suggestions that I hadn't considered.

The pace of life was slower and more relaxed. I was wrapped, surrounded—*inundated* by nature. Crisp mountain air swept across the expanses of land that glowed with sunlight and a sort of untouched perfection. I could put the search on the back-burner for a while. Relax. Not worry about it.

I was happy. And Colorado was no coincidence. One of my favorite T-shirts reads: "Coincidence is God's Way of Remaining Anonymous." I knew I was supposed to be there, even though Colorado would end up bringing a mix of personal joys, and a lot of career frustration. In the midst of my life in the mountains, I met friends who remain close to me today, realized a lifetime dream to live in such a setting, and ultimately made the decision to return to Oklahoma after losing a couple of jobs to a dreadful economy and a difficult mental-health employment environment.

Dhiana Clarice is a dear friend I met soon after my move to Colorado. As it turned out, she was instrumental in my search process. Dhiana is a loving, spiritually focused woman who suggested that I see a woman in Pueblo who could speak to people on the "other side." She had a remarkable reputation for being the "real deal." After hearing my story about Lillie and all I had been through, Dhiana felt certain this was something I had to do. I was not convinced. I felt like I'd had all the insight from "seers" I needed for a while. After all, when you are used to someone like Lillie, other clairvoyants pale in comparison.

Sometime in early 2001 I saw Monica Cervanyk for the first time, with considerable reservation and after much persuading from Dhiana.

As I sat down with Monica for the first time, she said, "I have someone here with me… she's an older woman, and she says that when you came to see her, there was a cat calendar on the wall to your right. She says she had long white hair but you only saw it up. It's funny…she's showing me an entire field of lilies. "

I was overcome with emotion, knowing immediately it was Lillie. My eyes welled with tears. Monica said: "Do you know who this is?" I nodded, a tear escaping my eye and rolling down one cheek.

"Lillie wants you to know that she is here."

Sadly, I knew that if she was "here," it meant she had died. I asked if she had passed on. Monica replied, "Lillie says yes, shortly after you moved to Colorado."

Monica went on to say that Lillie was being "very directive" about the reading, giving Monica information to pass on to me. Monica began telling me so many things, almost verbatim, that Lillie had told me over the years.

Lillie told Monica that, as a medium, she was "Good, but not as good as me!" Monica chuckled—amused, taking it all good-naturedly. I recognized that little quip as vintage Lillie —telling it exactly how she saw it, never mincing her words.

Monica conveyed a great deal of information. She talked about my biological family and my grandfather's grief over not finding me. She directed me to a history book, with a photo of a boat—even supplying the page number—where my grandfather was pictured on the deck in dress clothes and a top hat, with what appeared to be bales of cotton. (I never located the book.) If Monica would try to interject, Lillie would redirect and remind Monica that she was "running this reading." It was unbelievable. My head was spinning. I had left Oklahoma and was directed to a clairvoyant…who was then talking with Lillie! I had profound awareness that this journey, and the purpose behind it, was much bigger than me.

I left Monica's office with my mind racing. I searched the

mental archives of my very Presbyterian upbringing for some explanation. How does something like this happen? One dies, becomes an inhabitant of the "other side," and shows up at a clairvoyant's house in Colorado? How did Lillie know to find me there? Or did she steer me there? Did she help set it up, so to speak? I played through the synchronicities that had been layered in perfect unison to create the situation in which Lillie could communicate with me again. She had said "I will be with you until all of this comes to pass." How did she manage that? Was she now an angel? A guide? What did you call her and how did it all work? Perhaps it was her assignment. Or maybe it was just *love* and her desire to help me. Stranger than fiction? Absolutely. Who could make this up? If I hadn't been living it, I'd never have believed it.

Monica's journey into helping others as a clairvoyant was a fascinating one. She had started her career as a therapist—a Licensed Professional Counselor, but she had been very intuitive from birth. She sometimes even knew who was on the phone before it rang. Monica and her husband had started doing foster care. They were given an infant who had been terribly abused by his mother (who was fighting for the right to keep him), and they cared for him for about three years. You can imagine what kind of bond develops between a couple and an infant during three years of caregiving. They loved the child like their own and wanted to keep him, but the court kept going back and forth about whether to fully terminate parental rights. Throughout all the ups and downs of the legal wrangling, Monica and her husband had fallen more deeply in love with the child, and he became psychologically inextricable from their family.

Monica loathed the idea of visitation by the child's birth-mother, but there was nothing she could do—the court's decisions were law. The judge ordered what Monica and her legal team had hoped would be one final visit with the birth mom. The young boy was taken to see her, and during the visit, the birthmother killed him.

Monica was devastated beyond words. It was during this period that she started seeing and hearing people on the other side. She even saw her slain foster child. She didn't necessarily want this gift, but she accepted it. It took her a long time to figure out how to keep it from driving her crazy, but with practice and effort, she learned how she could essentially mentally turn the messages on and off. She also decided to donate all the money she received for her services to St. Jude's.

You couldn't go to her with a "call-sheet" and just ring up anyone you want. People came through to her, or they didn't. It was out of her control. It might be someone you would never expect to talk to. Other than Lillie, who was present during every reading, I had several people present to share something with me over the first couple of years I knew Monica.

Once she said, "There's someone here who's old enough to be your grandmother…she says she loves you very, very much…and you called her a one-syllable name. She wants me to tell you that she always reminded you to scrape the last little bit of egg out of the shell with your finger."

"Yes, that was my Gran," I acknowledged, again overcome with emotion.

Wow! That was astounding.

Gran had been so good to me. But my dad's parents, Grandmother and Grandfather Noonan had been exceedingly cruel. They constantly reminded people that I was not "blood." Given the option, they never would've acknowledged I even existed. But I was ninety-eight degrees, took up space in a room, and had a pulse—which were facts too indelible for them to disregard me altogether. Still, they never gave me the same attention as my brother. If there was something fun to do, they would take him but didn't want me. This was the kind of family drama that irritated my insecurities about being adopted.

Now Monica said, "There is someone here named Grace.

Do you know her?"

I replied "Yes, that was my dad's mother, Grace Noonan."
Monica said, "She wants to tell you how sorry she is for
the way she treated you." My first thought was, *Well, better
late than never.* I guess once you make it to the other side,
things become a bit clearer...and souls become kinder. Grace
asked if I could forgive her and I assured her I already had.

The readings with Monica were amazing in that Lillie picked
up where she'd been the last time I saw her alive...most of it
verbatim. The details continued to evolve and improve. During one reading, Monica remarked "I know of a woman who
does past-life work. It might benefit you to see her."

"Here we go again," I thought, while moaning aloud about
it. But Monica thought it might provide information for my
search, so I acquiesced. I couldn't argue about the brilliant
manner in which I'd been reunited with Lillie. Maybe this was
one more thing I was supposed to do.

My appointment was two weeks later. I walked into a
room that was divided in two. One side had two chairs with a
table between them, the other had a larger table with chairs
that slid under it. It was very homey and quaint, really.

I went in and met the practitioner, and she was very kind.
She said, "Do you have in your mind what you want to know?"

"Not really, I just want to investigate...whatever's going
to happen."

"Come over here." I sat down across from her at a small
table. "Give me your hand," she said, and as I did so a bizarre
look raced across her face. She broke down—weeping, sobbing.

Now, how would you feel if you presented your hand to a
clairvoyant, and she started weeping?

"I'm sorry," she said, "I don't know if I can do this, I'll be
glad to give your money back... it's your mother, what they
did to her was terrible."

I was freaked out. I thought either this woman is some kind of weirdo or things aren't looking good for me. How could she go from zero to breakdown in ten seconds?

Again she offered a refund: "I just don't know that I can do this. I'll be glad to give you the seventy-five dollars back."

I asked her at least to tell me what was so horrible.

"It's something like an insane hospital," she said. "It was someplace where she was locked up. And she knew if she didn't do what they said, she'd never get out."

So now I was thinking, this woman has no clue I'm adopted. Then she said, "Let me try something else... let me do it this way...."

And she reached for her cards. She started laying them out, and said: "There's a man coming through here who's old. And he's standing in a cemetery. It's a very old cemetery, and he's in what looks to be a dress military uniform...He's very animated and very excited. 'You have no idea who you are, you have no idea who you are, you have no idea your family's place in history.' He's saying this."

Then she said, "He's almost literally jumping up and down."

A moment later, she said, "You know, I think he's English or Scottish."

I didn't have a clue who he was.

"He just wants you to know how important your family was in history. He just keeps telling me that over and over and over...."

After that whole deal was finished, we moved into more casual conversation. "Can you tell me anything at all about what I just saw? Why I saw it?" she asked.

"Well, I'm adopted. I've been trying for many years to find my grandpa. I don't know who that was, but I'm wondering if that was him."

She said: "Something horrible happened to your mother. Have you found her?"

"No."

"I don't know what it was, but it's like she was threatened, and definitely afraid. She knew that whoever these people were, you were not supposed to cross them... it would be bad." And that was the troubling, yet vitally important result of my time with her. It was very powerful. She was extremely sweet and very kind through it all.

I was now living and working in Colorado Springs. Mom and Dad lived across the street from Aunt Jo. They had sold their house in Tonkawa and moved out to Colorado full time. I was glad because Dad's health was declining, and I wanted to be closer to him.

Early on Christmas Eve, Mom woke up and found Dad on the floor next to the bed. She called me and said, "I think your dad is dead."

"I'll be right there." And I got in the car.

Disbelief. Shock.

It took me about twenty minutes to get to their house. I walked in and saw Dad's body. I hadn't seen a dead person since high school. He was lying half on his side. I was profoundly impacted by how evident, how clear it was that he had "left the building." My dad was at peace. Undeniably so.

The coroner came, then the funeral director's men came and took the body. Jim came from Oklahoma a couple of days later. The whole thing was surreal.

Mom knew how he had suffered. She didn't cry much in our presence. I think she was ready for it in a way—because he was ready to be done.

A few months later I saw Monica, and my Dad came through. "He's asking you to take a message to your mother," Monica said.

By the time Dad had died, he had quit sleeping in the same bed with Mom, because he had trouble breathing. Now

Mom was beating herself up because she hadn't heard him in his final distress. He had fallen between the bed and wall, and she thought he most likely fell while he was trying to get her attention, and she didn't respond.

That idea haunted her. She always feared and regretted that he essentially died alone in the next room—unable to get a last communication out to her. But now Dad was reassuring her—through Monica: "Tell her that she did everything right, and I am fine, that I love her very much, and I am not gone, and that she needs to live her life."

That's all he said, and then he was gone. He said nothing to me. Not a word. He just wanted me to communicate his message to Mom.

Dad, Gran, and Dad's mother are the only three other people who ever came through to Monica.

Those three, and Lillie.

After Dad died, Mom decided that she would live with me, and I was thrilled about it. But it wasn't long after that that I got laid off, which put a lot of pressure on our domestic relationship. Mom was frustrated and I was annoyed that I couldn't find work. All of this was unfolding in the shadow of my lost father. It was very difficult time for us. We decided to move back to Oklahoma and into a new place in a town called Claremore. I knew many people in and around Tulsa and felt sure I could easily find a good job.

It was around this time that one of the Oklahoma state legislators decided she wanted to have a community forum on the issue of adoption search, so there was a town-hall meeting. There were a couple of judges, lawyers, DHS workers, and a smattering of adult adoptees. Everyone was invited to attend. I was excited to be going to my first real legislative event regarding adoption.

It was held in an auditorium downtown, and they had six speakers. People came with questions. I was nervous about saying anything, so I just watched. Seeing all these adult adoptees gathered together resonated deeply in me. Some were young—barely in their twenties; others were in their seventies. They stood patiently in line to speak, and everyone's voice was heard. It was a solemn spectacle.

The emotional tone struck by the adoptees was one of suppliant anguish. They talked about the hurdles they'd encountered in their own lives, and how desperately they wanted to uncover the most basic information about their histories; they sounded as though they were begging for their lives. They started out composed—gliding through the first two or three sentences of their prepared notes—and then their voices cracked and tears ran like faucets. It was one of the oddest and most heart-rending experiences I had ever had. It felt like the very air had been sucked out of the room.

Tangible.

Heavy.

Suffocating.

Raw.

*Grief.*

Welcome to the world of closed-record adoptions.

"It is no use saying 'we are doing our
best.' You have got to succeed in doing
what is necessary."

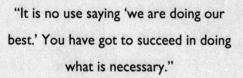

*Winston Churchill*

# 9

# "Uncertain, hazardous, and conflicting information"

About six months prior to leaving Colorado, I phoned Debra Goodman, the new head of the Reunion Registry, and requested a search for my biological father. She pulled out my case and said, "I don't want to discourage you, but this would be like finding a needle in a haystack. We have very little to go on, and it's a very common name in a very big city."

I didn't ask her where she got the name, I just requested their best searcher, and she assured me I would get exactly that and that they would be looking in the northeast.

After several weeks she called to say they had "a list of the top six possibilities but no one who is definite." She said they had phoned about seventy-five people with the name they had, and that the searcher had been working hard on it. That was in November 2004.

Margaret Daniel took over the case as the new head of the intermediary program. She agreed to look my birthmother up every six months to make sure she was still alive. If she died, I would be able to connect with my half-sisters—because the legal issue of "privacy" doesn't extend to the grave.

I phoned Margaret in early July to ask her to check on my biological mom again. About a week passed and she phoned to say she was still alive, was living with one of my half-sisters, and seemed to be doing well. (I don't know how she could know that, if all she was doing was checking the Social Security death index. Perhaps it was just an assumption because my mother had been ill—the first time the intermediary had found her, she had some health problems—and was still alive.)

Margaret also said that the man they believed to be my biological father had called the intermediary and was going to call back, further explaining that he seemed "paranoid" about what I wanted, and asked several times if I had found or talked to my biological mom yet. She said he clearly stated that he did not want to go on with contact if I had found and/ or contacted my biological mother.

She said he was supposed to call back. The following morning Margaret phoned and asked for the number at which I wanted him to call me, and about thirty minutes later a man phoned my house.

His name was Robert Ray Schultz, of New Braunfels, Texas (just outside of Greene, where he actually lived). He told me he was 5'11" tall and 180 pounds (exactly what was in my non-identifying information); that he worked as a border patrol agent for the government, and traveled a lot. He was of German/Dutch ancestry; both his parents lived into their late eighties. He had been widowed twice (his first wife was more than twenty years his junior; his second was an educational leader in Nebraska, and died during a surgery in 1997). His health was good; he'd had an aorta replacement; and was 77 years old.

He said that he did not know my birthmother. He'd been driving from Nebraska to Texas and stopped for the night in Oklahoma City. He got a room in the downtown area, and the hotel help advised him he could go down an alley and around a corner, and if he lit a cigarette, that would be the signal required to be ushered into a speakeasy where bootleggers had liquor flowing.

He met two "very attractive women"—my mother and a friend—at the bar and began talking. About two minutes into the conversation, my biological mother asked if he had a car and could take her home. He agreed, and escorted her to a simple but clean and neat apartment. He said there were no children there, and he remembered her saying she worked at Tinker.

Tinker Air Force base is legendary in Oklahoma. It covers nine square miles, has 760 buildings, and boasts more than 26,000 military and civilian employees. It's also the largest single-site employer in the state of Oklahoma.

In 1940 the War Department was considering the central United States as a location for a supply and maintenance depot. Tinker Field was the result. It was the site of a Douglas Aircraft factory that produced half of the C-47 Skytrains used in World War II. Another, perhaps greater, claim to fame is that on September 29, 1957, Buddy Holly recorded "An Empty Cup, " "Rock Me My Baby, " "You've Got Love, " and "Maybe Baby" in the Tinker Air Force Base Officers' Club. It was a happening place for all kinds of government bigshots and entertainment stars. They would drink and dance and carouse into the wee hours. The base sits right next to Oklahoma City—a large metropolis and the state capital. So Tinker was quickly and easily accessible to anyone visiting the machines of state government.

Robert Schultz continued to tell me about my mom, and about the story relayed to him by DHS.

"There is one thing that doesn't match up. They say I met her in the Officers' Club at Tinker and I've never been in the Officers' Club at Tinker. We met in a bar and I took her home."

He claimed he did not remember her name but recalled very specific information about the events of that night. "I remember feeling like I might have been set up. It was strange. She was a very attractive woman, and clearly not a streetwalker."

Schultz had one son, a merchant marine, from whom he was currently estranged. His son had one daughter, age eleven. He talked about his son's marital problems for a while, too. He then said he would like to come see me, and told me he could come within the next two weeks. He said he would stay a few days. I offered the house and he said, "Whatever you want."

He asked if I would be DNA tested; and I said, "Yes, of course."

He inquired if I lived alone and I told him no. He said he would call back in a day or two when he knew his schedule. Two days later, he phoned and I missed his call. I called back and he said he couldn't come in August but that he could come on September 16 if that was all right. He would stay at the Super 8 and leave the next morning. He also mentioned that he wanted to see the Will Rogers Museum while he was here, and would "take you and your mama out to dinner."

He asked me what my height and weight were, and offered his stats in return: "I am 6'1" and 195 pounds. I used to be 6'2" but I think I've shrunk a little as I've gotten older, and I used to weigh 210, but I've lost fifteen pounds."

He again asked if I lived alone, and I told him again what I had told him before. He said he would call when he got to town in September but to feel free to call anytime.

As I replayed the conversation in my mind, I was perplexed at the differences in his height and weight from our previous conversation. He seemed to be quoting the non-identifying information about the birthfather and then giving other numbers. I wondered if this man had been in on the conspiracy to hide my identity all along. Perhaps he had been "selected" as the person to leave the bar with my birthmother, in front of her friend, so others would believe that he was actually the father. Maybe he was simply playing me, wondering what I had found out; if I knew anything. I did not trust him.

September breezed in and Robert Schultz materialized, as promised. He was very kind, very gracious, and exceedingly polite. He explained all sorts of things to me; firstly, and most importantly: "I'm not your dad, but I would've loved to have you as a daughter, and I wish I could help you find who you're looking for."

He went on to explain precisely how and why he couldn't be my father.

"I had just bought a car when I met your mother. I had detailed records of it, and it was right before Christmas. So that was two months too late."

Schultz also reported men following him and his date from the bar that night. "I was afraid I'd stepped in it," he said a few times.

He told me detailed stories about what had happened forty-five years earlier, and said he had replayed them over and over in his mind because it was clear to him that the woman wasn't a prostitute. Back in those days men didn't just pick women up in a bar that easily. We talked and talked, and ended dinner, and went back to our lives.

It was several days after his visit that my Mom and I were chatting, and she said, out of the blue, "You know the FBI talked with your grandparents, don't you?"

I was surprised, but not shocked. I asked mom why she hadn't told me before. She said, "I guess I just never thought about it," and told me of my Gran phoning her at the bank (where she had worked as a teller) to say the agents had interviewed both her and Grandpa as well as three other businessmen in town. When Mom asked why they were visited by FBI agents, Gran said that she thought it had "something to do with you wanting to adopt a baby...I guess they are just checking on that." Some fifteen years earlier, Lillie had told me the FBI had been involved—and I had wondered if she'd lost her mind. Guess not.

I knew I had to file a request under the Freedom of Information Act. If the FBI had been involved, there should be a record somewhere—wouldn't you think? I did all the research online, learned about the forms, and submitted all the necessary paperwork. I even sent the required death certificates and other attachments.

I waited, and waited, and waited.

Finally I got frustrated and phoned. I don't know if you've ever tried to just up and call the FBI, but it's not an easy task. Ultimately I talked to some people in D.C. who put me in touch with an FBI agent who worked at the Pentagon.

I told him what I was trying to find out: that I knew the FBI had been in Tonkawa at the time I was referencing. He said, "It might have been FBI...or might not have been." He basically said the FBI would have had nothing to do with an adoption unless it involved a foreign dignitary or a foreign diplomat.

*Bingo!* I thought.

On Thursday night an old friend of mine from college, Cathy O'Dell was visiting at the house in Claremore. We searched online for "Irene Pruitt." Ancestry.com was up and running by that time, and through it we found Irene Pruitt on the 1930 census—in Murray County, Oklahoma.

The next day, she and I drove out to Murray County and actually found the land where Irene Pruitt lived with her parents when the 1930 census was taken. But when we arrived it was totally desolate.

We knocked on doors and talked to strangers we spotted. We found one woman who was 97 years old, still living in that area, and who had been there all her life. She actually remembered an "Irene" who lived there as a child, but who was now long gone.

It had to be my birthmother.

I felt like I had come so far, only to reach another dead end. So I threw myself back into my job. I was working tirelessly to put the final polish on an adoption seminar I was teaching in Chicago. If I couldn't help myself, I could always help others.

"People will be proud of you and
will watch you. Their language—
your people—is all wadded up...
from another country.
Lots of history in your family.
Your grandfather traveled.
He went all over the world."

———

*Lillie, 1995*

**10**

# "The equal sharing of miseries"

F rom my personal journal: "I arrived at O'Hare on a brisk Friday in November. The yellow clouds blazed gold and orange, then rubied, and surrendered to twilight during my ride into the city."

The plane trip was spent studying notes and preparing for my presentation. I had given more of these than I could count. DHS departments had lively educational sessions and speakers in many specialties: ADHD, abuse, play therapy, psychotropic meds, bipolar disorder in children, foster care, parenting techniques, and so on.

Cook County isn't exactly a beginner's course in children and family services and interventions. Chicago is a huge city with a massive department. These people were the best of the best, and perhaps faced with some of the toughest challenges in these areas.

My topic? "Truth in Adoption."

By now, I'd devoted much of my life to the subject.

Saturday morning. The clock fastidiously ticked off the hours as I dressed, enjoyed breakfast and coffee, and prepared for the day.

Arriving at DHS I was pleased to see about 150 people had shown up. Many of them were child welfare workers, responsible for Cook Country children taken into custody. There was also a nice mix of counselors, caseworkers, and therapists, peppered with a few lawyers and adoption agency employees. It was a great crowd—affable and good-humored, especially considering the stress these jobs place on people.

I was introduced.

"Good morning everyone. Glad to see you all here today. I'd like to introduce today's speaker. Rhonda Noonan is the Clinical Director of Shadow Mountain Hospital, an in-patient psychiatric facility in Tulsa, Oklahoma. Rhonda is the coordinator of the Adoption/Attachment Disorder Treatment track."

I took the podium and delivered my speech, the text of which follows.

*Good morning. I'm really delighted to be here today, and before I start, I'd like to let you know, if you have any questions, don't hesitate to interrupt me. I appreciate having a discussion with any of you.*

*Today I'm going to talk about adoption, and I hope to dispel a few myths about adoption and about every member of the adoption triad: the adoptees, the families, and the birthparents. Let's start the larger discussion by talking about open records.*

*The big legal debate over the past few years has been over the level of access each member of the adoption triad should have. There's been a national debate, and there is now a proposal pending in Congress for a National Voluntary Reunion Registry. At the state level, bills are also being introduced that would allow adopted adults access to their original birth certificates.*

*Now, there have been two main arguments raised against these efforts, and you've probably heard them. First, that adopted adults and their birthparents don't wish to be found by each other, so they don't need their records. Second, that adoptive parents are opposed to their adopted children having that information.*

*But what many people don't know is that there is a solid body of research refuting these arguments.*

*The data say quite clearly that both birthparents and adopted adults do want to be found by each other. In 1989, the Maine Department of Human Resources Task Force on Adoption did a comprehensive study of adoption issues which found an overwhelming desire to be found by both sides.*

*Maine's DHS admitted it was "startled" to discover how few people didn't want to be found. Here's what they found: of 130 birthparents surveyed, all 130 wanted to be found by the child they had placed for adoption. And of the 164 adoptees surveyed, 95 percent expressed a desire to be found by their parents. In 1991, Paul Sachdev did a study that showed 85.5 percent of birthmothers and 81.1 percent of adoptees support adult adoptees having access to records identifying their birthparents.*

*To be sure, practice-based knowledge further validates that birthparents and adoptees want to be found by one another. Contrary to the assertion that birthparents move on with their lives, and live in fear that the children they relinquished for adoption will intrude upon them, research and the work with birthparents undertaken by Becker in 1989, Demick and Wapner in 1988, and Baran, Pannor and Sorosky in 1976, uniformly finds that birthparents do not forget the children they relinquished for adoption, wonder whether they are alive and healthy and express strong desires to be found by them; and also finds that the grief they experience in having relinquished their children is intensified by the secrecy surrounding adoption and the walls the adoption system has erected against any contact.*

*Rosemary Avery's 1996 research on the attitudes of adoptive parents in New York regarding access to identifying information found that 84 percent of the adoptive mothers and 73 percent of the adoptive fathers agreed or strongly agreed that an adult adoptee should be able to obtain identifying information on his or her birthparents.*

*This research reflects higher levels of support than that found in Feiglemen and Silverman's 1986 research on the attitudes of adoptive parents.*

*That study—more than ten years old—nevertheless found that 55 percent of the adoptive parents of American-born children supported legislation easing restrictions on their children learning about their birth families, while 66 percent of adoptive parents of internationally adopted children expressed their support.*

*In conclusion, the research basically makes it clear that birthparents and adopted adults both want access to identifying information; and, adoptive families, rather than feeling threatened by their children's needs and interest in their birth families, support that access.*

*Other research, including that done by McRoy and Grotevant in 1994, demonstrates that benefits flow to all members of the triad when information is more freely shared and there is greater openness in relationships. Policies that facilitate connections between birth families and adopted adults and access to information, have strong empirical and practical support.*

*Now, on to the most important part of my talk today: Adoption myths.*

*Whenever changes occur in social policy, resistance is offered by those who believe and practice the current or former system. Before adoptee access to the original birth certificate was legislated in certain places, hard data existed regarding the impact of information being given to adopted persons.*

*The results based on states that have instituted adoption reform and recorded in hard data, allow us to shatter the following myths:*

*Myth Number One: Only a small number of adopted people want to know their birth information.*

*In a study of American adolescents, the Search Institute found that 72 percent of adopted adolescents wanted to know why they were adopted; 65 percent wanted to meet their birthparents; and 94 percent wanted to know which of their birthparents they looked like.*

*Psychological literature has established that whether mental or actual, searching is understandable and common, and part of healthy adaptation for adopted people. (See* A Psychosocial Model of Adoption Adjustment *by David Brodzinsky, Marshall Schechter, and Robin Marantz Henig.)*

*In Oregon, as of February 1, 2007, seven years after passage of approving access in 2000, 9,193 adult adoptees have requested, and 8,878 have received, their original birth certificates.*

*Myth Number Two: Most birthmothers want to forget the past and not have "old wounds reopened."*

*Through registries and data collected in states and countries where access was legislated, 95 percent of birthparents who were contacted wanted reunion. In Oregon, only 0.25 percent of birthparents requested no contact.*

*Myth Number Three: Birthmothers need to be protected from searching adoptees.*

*Birthparents have the same protections under the law as anyone else. They have the right of privacy and boundaries as does everyone, but privacy does not equal secrecy. Privacy is about healthy boundaries; secrecy prevents people from having information about themselves.*

*John Triseliotis, a researcher from the University of Edinburgh, found in 25 years of study that adoptees needed genealogical and background information to confirm their identities based on both adoptive and birth families. In researching the impact of opening records in Great Britain, he found those who did search "did so with considerable forethought. Furthermore, the vast majority are over-careful not to hurt anyone's feelings."* (*See* In Search of Origins: The Experience of Adopted People *by John Triseliotis, Routledge and Kegan Paul, January 1, 1973.)*

*Ninety-four percent of non-searching birthmothers were pleased when contacted by their adult birthchildren, according to a recent British study.* (*See* The Adoption Triangle Revisited: A Study of Adoption Search and Reunion Experiences, *British Association for Adoption and Fostering, 2005.)*

*Myth Number Four: Lifting secrecy will increase abortion.*

*Data from states where access exists reveals that if it has had any effect on adoptions and abortions, it was to increase adoptions and decrease abortions. Since adult adoptees in Oregon and Alabama obtained access to their original birth certificates in 2000, abortions have declined much faster in those states than in the nation as a whole.*

*Between then and 2003, resident abortions declined 10 percent in Oregon and 13 percent in Alabama, but only 2 percent in the nation as a whole. In other words, after adoptees gained access in those states, abortions declined five times as fast as in the country as a whole.*

*Workers at pro-life centers such as Birthright report that young women today will only choose adoption if they are assured of updates or contact with the adoptive family. Gretchen Traylor, a Birthright counselor in Minnesota, says "When adoption is under consideration, the young woman's overriding concern is that she will be unable to contact her child later in life, and that the child will not be able to find her as well. Pregnant women tell me that if such contact is not available, they would rather abort."*

*In a national survey of 1,900 women having abortions, not one woman cited the inability to choose a confidential adoption as a factor in her decision to have the abortion. (See "Reasons for Terminating an Unwanted Pregnancy," Guttmacher Institute, 2003.)*

*A September 24, 2004 Wall Street Journal article reports that those parts of the country practicing open adoption currently do not have enough couples to adopt infants being relinquished by birthparents wanting open adoption.*

*Myth Number Five: Opening up adoption records will break up adoptive families.*

*"With a law that gives adults access to their original birth certificates, nothing changes while the adoptee is a child under the care of adoptive parents. Birth information and contact with the birth family does not replace one's relationship to adoptive parents, but rather leads to a more cohesive identity for some adult adoptees.*

*Research from the United Kingdom on the results of access found that the loyalty and love adopted peo-*

*ple felt toward their adoptive parents and family did not lessen as a result of the search and reunion process. In some cases, adopted people reported that the experience of searching enhanced their relationship with their adoptive families.* (British Association for Adoption and Fostering, *2004.)*

*After New Zealand allowed adult adoptee access to adoption records, researchers found that reunions actually strengthened relationships between adoptees and their adoptive parents, often laying fantasies about the birth family to rest. Results showed that adopted children and adults can successfully integrate two or more families into their lives. Finding birth relatives does not mean they relinquish their adoptive ones. (See* The Right to Know Who You Are, *Keith C. Griffith)*

*Research conducted by the University of Minnesota and University of Texas reveals that parental fears about entitlement in open adoptions were unfounded, and in many ways, contact with the birth family strengthened the bond between adoptive parents and children. (See* Openness in Adoption, *Harold D. Grotevant and Ruth G. McRoy.)*

*Myth Number Six: Adoptees conceived by rape or incest (and birthmothers too) will be devastated by search, reunion, and/or learning the truth about their origins.*

*While unsavory details of one's past are not pleasant to cope with, they still are a part of one's life. Denying access to someone's personal information is robbing that person of his or her heritage. The contents of the information are not as important as the fact that information becomes available, and questions are able to be answered.*

*New Zealand found that adult adoptees can bet-*

*ter cope with such traumatic revelations than with not having any information at all. Interestingly enough, many had already fantasized the event. Most adoptees know that in exploring the unknown void of their origins, anything is possible, and realize that there must have been difficulties or they would not have been placed for adoption. This information remaining secret increases the shame. The reality, once it is confronted, is less than the enormity of the secret.*

*One adoptee conceived from rape said of his birthmother, "When we met things were pretty tense between us. I knew that she was holding back something. I asked her and she told me. We both held each other tight and wept for almost an hour. Then we shared exactly what had happened and we shared our hurts and fears....It was one of my birthmother's fears that one day I would find her and ask her. And now that traumatic time had come. Somehow, in the sharing of our deep personal grief feelings, we built up a relationship. We now understand each other on an issue that no one else seems to understand."*

*You will hear all of these myths repeated as conventional wisdom by the overwhelming majority of Americans.*

*But they are false, and the overwhelming majority of Americans are suffering under their deceptive and erroneous influence.*

I broke from my notes throughout the presentation to engage with the audience; but I can't recall the interactions verbatim. These meetings are always very lively. People are shocked to discover that their trusted assumptions aren't based on anything in reality or truth.

I loved the starlit gaze of enlightenment that swept over

the faces of the audience. I realized that many people never even think about the word "adoption," much less get tangled up in its tricky, sticky triad. Most people had just swallowed what was called "conventional wisdom" about the subject, and now they realized their view of the world was backwards.

I took deep satisfaction in dispelling all these lies—as they were the fuel for the machine that haunted my life.

"It is better to do
the wrong thing than to do
nothing."

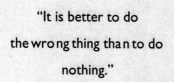

*Winston Churchill*

# 11

## *"In defeat: defiance"*

I was living in Wagoner, and Margaret Daniel was head of adoption services for Oklahoma. I phoned her and said I wanted to discuss some discrepancies in my case. She agreed to meet with me in person. On the appointed day I loaded up the car, and Mom and I headed back to the Sequoyah Building in Oklahoma City.

Margaret met me in a conference room. I had my court records, my original birth certificate—my entire file. I told Margaret what Bonnie Walton had said to me years before—that there was a hint in that file as to the identity of my actual biological father—and asked her if she would look for it.

She had on the table what she said was my DHS file, and she showed me a blackened piece of paper–copied microfiche—and at the top it said "Biological Father" and had Robert Schultz's name and limited identifying information. She commented that it was the document that had been in the file all along.

"So, as far as this department is concerned, Robert Schultz is my biological father?" I asked.

"Yes." (This answer would play a critical role in a later legal move.)

I explained to her that I had actually met Robert Schultz, and told her what I had learned from him: that he didn't hook up with Irene Pruitt until Christmas of the year prior to my birth. So he met her when she was two months pregnant, and he knew this because he worked for the Federal Border Pa-

trol, and kept detailed logs. The logs reflected he had just purchased a car in Nebraska, and was on his way home to Texas
when he stopped in Oklahoma–just before Christmas.

I asked Margaret to scour my file for any suggestion of
another man, or for a comment that didn't seem to fit Schultz;
perhaps it was someone of political notoriety or who was otherwise well-known. For years Lillie had told me that I had a
"high-profile" father; I imagined perhaps someone tied to the
governor's office, or maybe some state judge or other Oklahoma City heavy-hitter.

I told Margaret about the FBI visiting Tonkawa, and
about the comment made to my grandmother from the caseworker when I was adopted. I told her Schultz's version of
what happened—with the men following him—and the fact
that my parents' phone was surely tapped as they could never
call "the city" from another one.

All of this seemed to have pointed to somebody of some
significance. "Please scour my file to find someone else's
name." I asked again.

She said she would, and she did, and said, "I just don't see
anything here at all."

Margaret was very compassionate and helpful; very kind.
We wrapped up our meeting and collected our things to leave;
and as we did so she revealed that she was adopted herself. In
fact it had been just a few days since she had learned who her
own parent was, and she strongly agreed that the laws should
change; that it should be easier for children to find their parents.

Several mornings later, I got out of bed and went into the
bathroom. As I began to brush my teeth I looked in the mir-
ror and noticed, behind me, a perfectly outlined handprint on
one of my towels. I keep a pretty neat house, especially the
bathroom. The towel was clean and fluffed, and neatly folded
and hung precisely over the towel rack. It was a heavy, deep-

navy blue designer towel, and it was "embossed" with this handprint—a sort of powdery grey shade. Its alignment was fingers-up, and diagonal. It looked like someone had stuck a hand in finely powdered laundry soap, then made a perfect print. I knew it hadn't been there the previous evening, or I would have seen it while brushing my teeth before bed. It was obvious. You couldn't miss it.

I like to take baths, so I hadn't taken a shower in a week, and I knew that no one else had used the bathroom. I was mystified by that handprint. I asked my two roommates: "Have you guys been in my bathroom?"

"No."

"Have you used any of my towels?"

"Nope!"

I told them about the handprint. It was absolutely perplexing. I could not figure out how it had happened. Then, as I was driving to work, I remembered how Lillie would hold my hands up and place hers against mine. I decided that handprint must have had something to do with Lillie. At that very moment, I turned on my radio, to hear a news piece announcing the Federal Reserve was going to start printing currency with colored ink. "Hello, my friend," I said aloud, looking towards the Heavens.

Lillie had said in 1988: "I can tell you when this will start—it will start in the time of the colored money."

I grew tired of the longer-than-necessary commute to Tulsa and the added distance from Mom. So I moved. I found acreage in Sand Springs, Oklahoma—a full hour closer to Tonkawa, and to Mom. I loaded up Bubba, Cowboy, and Boomer (two Appaloosas and a paint—I had been adding to my stable), plus all my stuff, and moved into the house of my dreams. One whole side of the house was glass windows facing into the woods. The living room was a two-story atrium, and there was a den in the back, a barn, a long private drive. My life was going well. My career was flourishing, I was enjoying my role as a clinical director. I was doing some educational speaking engagements on adoption and attachment work. The Department of Mental Health asked me to speak at their respite weekend for adoptive parents. This was offered for parents who had adopted through the DHS system. I provided a three-hour attachment disorder training seminar, including a module on parenting tools for adopted kids.

Through that network I had gotten to know folks who worked in post-adoptive services for the state. I was also invited to be part of a task force that studied adoption services for the State of Oklahoma. I mentioned some of my struggles to one of the women I had met in post-adoptive services, and asked if I could come down and talk to her one-on-one. She obliged.

So there I went (which could be the title of half my life), back to the Sequoyah Building. I explained all the inconsistencies in my case and asked for her opinion. I was hoping at that point there was something, anything, I could do to move my search forward—that maybe someone on the inside could help me out.

I said, "Look, basically I requested my file, and you sent me an updated 'non-identifying information' sheet. That is not my file. Even the blackened piece of microfiche that Margaret Daniel held up should have been in there. Every piece of documentation should have been in there." I explained to her that I wanted to see that microfiche copy about Robert Schultz—in case it contained clues to something else.

She said, "There wasn't much there. We gave you everything that we have, but I'll double-check." Then she vanished into the back. She quickly reappeared, and said, "Yeah, you have it all."

I just leveled with her. "The thing that frustrates me the most, is that all these years I've been told different things. I have fought for everything... court records, an original

birth certificate, my official file. I have my mother's name…
or somebody's name, but if you don't know if any of the names
on any of the documents are correct, then how do you know
who to look for?"

She replied, "That was her name—when you were adopted. I don't think that's her name any more."

THAT WAS HER NAME. Yay! Finally.

Something to go on. It was a start.

She added, "I can give you the number of a woman in Tulsa who has helped kids find their biological parents. Her name
is Linda Colvard."

I got up and left, and as I was driving I grabbed my phone.
I thought to myself, after all these years of nothing, it's not
likely this woman would be able to provide me anything new.
But I called her anyway. She answered, and I explained a bit
about myself.

"I would love to meet with you and talk to you," she said.
"I'll need all your records."

I said, "I've got them all with me. I'm on my way back
from DHS right now, and if you're free now, I'll come right to
your house."

"Fine. I look forward to seeing you."

I drove directly to her without stopping. Linda lived in a
beautiful house—perfectly appointed and immaculate, with a
gigantic yard on a quiet street. I stayed at least an hour—just
talking about my situation and her work. I told her that I had
just come from Oklahoma City and had confirmed that this was
my birthmother's name at the time of my adoption. She kept
the documents with the promise she'd give them back to me.

I soon discovered Linda was a genius, and knew more
about libraries and research than anyone I had ever met. She
was absolutely flabbergasted by how technical and long and
thorough my search had been.

As impressive as she was, I was at best cautiously optimistic about her ability to make any progress. After thirty years of searching and having court orders laughed at by the people who were hired to serve the public, I thought I would gladly give this woman a try, but I really didn't expect anything.

Still, she was so thorough and attentive and specific about what she needed and wanted. "Many times," she explained, "there are little hints that might not mean anything to you, but could be very important for my search." I left her home around five o'clock.

The following morning, around eleven, she called and said, "I don't want to get your hopes too high, but there is a very good chance I have located your biological mother." I could not believe my ears.

What I didn't know about Linda at that time was that she would never tell anyone "I found them" until she knew for sure. So she was waiting on one more piece of corroborating information from a librarian somewhere.

*Is she kidding me?* I thought. After I spent thirty years of fighting with bureaucrats and wandering through wheat fields, this woman found my mother in one night?—*without leaving home?*

"I'll be there as soon as I can," I promised, my heart pounding.

I flew straight into work to prepare for a big meeting scheduled for two o'clock, but then Linda called back at quarter to two with the confirmation she had been waiting for. *There is no way I can do this meeting*, I thought. So I told my boss, "They just found my birthmother—after I've been searching for her for thirty years. Can I go, please? I need to drive straight to Purcell, Oklahoma."

My boss was unmoved. He refused permission.

I sat anxiously through the two o'clock meeting—which dragged on to 3:30—then blew out of the parking lot like Secretariat out of the gate. I drove straight to Linda's house.

She was waiting for me, and said she had gotten confirmation of her suspicions as far as my birthmother having re-married. She believed my mother was living with her oldest daughter, Zelpha, a.k.a. Zippy—my half-sister!—and Zippy's husband, Bob.

Linda handed me a whole set of papers. One was a newspaper clipping about a car wreck another sister had been in years ago; my sisters' names; addresses, and phone numbers; and details about their marriages and divorces (and my mother's as well).

I did, indeed, have four half-sisters. That much was true! She then told me that my mother's name was now Pat Nail. Linda was a genius, and proof of the power of solid library research skills.

My heart was in my throat.

The moment was surreal.

I flashed back to a recurring dream I used to have—where there was a document that a woman was supposed to sign—I could see her face, but she would never write her name. As soon as she would start to sign, the paper would disintegrate, or her face would vanish or be obscured. I would strive so hard to read that name, gaze so intently at the page—just waiting for her to sign. Please sign it, sign it, sign it, so I can see what your name is. I had that dream many times in my life.

I returned to my car and headed to the address Linda gave me—in Purcell. I was not going to let another day pass —not another night, not another hour. I was not going to lie down to rest or sleep until I knocked on her door.

It was a summer evening, around seven, when I arrived— bright and sunny and hot—in fact scorching hot. I found the house and circled the block a couple of times, taking in the whole scene. It was a small place, very much like the one I grew up in. Very much like the neighborhood I grew up in, too. I pulled into the gravel driveway, nervous, sweating, and sat...because I had no idea what I was going to say.

I wanted to see her face. I wanted to look her in the eye. And

I wanted her to know that in spite of all her efforts to hide, her attempts to thwart my quest—despite all the lies, the lawyers, the social workers, the politicians, the decoys, the deception, the organized conspiracy of identity theft, the system of idiocy and immorality that had robbed me of my history, that gargantuan and hideous machinery of government designed to steal the knowledge of my very genetic ancestry and obliterate the Truth from history...I wanted to look her in the face and tell her: *I FOUND YOU.*

I sat in the driveway in a state of disbelief. I had nothing prepared. The only thing I was certain of was that I didn't want to leave until I got my father's name.

As I got out of the car I imagined it would be Zippy answering the door. With my birthmother's advanced age, I did not expect she would be the first one I would talk to. Mentally, I prepared accordingly.

I walked toward the front of the house—totally focused on that door. I knocked.

The door opened.

I knew instantly that it was my mother standing there staring me in the face—for the first time in fifty-two years. I looked at the shape of her face and mouth. More than any feature, it was the whole countenance that was manifestly related to my own. She opened the door about a foot, and spoke:

"Can I help you?

"Yes." I took a deep breath, then said, "Does July 8, 1956, mean anything to you?"

"Excuse me?" she responded, with a concerned and slightly puzzled look.

"I was born on July 8 in 1956. Does that mean anything to you?"

There was a pause. And she exhaled and asked, "So what do we do now?"

I heard a man's voice—Bob, Zippy's husband—speak from

inside the house. "Mom, who is it?"

"It's alright, I've got it," she said, and he said nothing more.

"Well," I said, and after an achingly long pause, "how have you been?"

"I've had my ups and downs," she responded. "You live in Tulsa?"

"Yeah, I do."

"What do you do for a living?"

"I'm a therapist. I actually work with a lot of adopted people and their families."

There was a long pause. I broke the silence with the reason I was there: "I know that you don't want to see me. I don't want to make trouble for you. The main thing I want to know is who my father is. Will you tell me?"

"No." She said it unhesitatingly, flatly. The quickness and definite nature of her refusal caught me offguard.

"Why not?" I asked.

"I was seeing a couple of men at the time, and I don't who it was."

"Well, give me both their names then."

"No. Nobody knows. None of my girls knows, and no one in the community knows, and I want it to stay that way."

At this point, I really didn't know what to do or say. What should I do—what *could* I do—about this stubborn little 92-year old woman? I was totally flummoxed. Should I rush the door? Barge in? Should I shout into the house? Call out to my sister? Say something—anything?

This was a critical moment in time and I didn't want to act hastily. In a soft, resolute voice, I said, "I have come this far. I mean you no harm. I will not stop until I find out who he is. Have a very nice evening."

I walked back to the car, my heart pounding and my mind racing. The best option, I decided, was to go back to Tulsa and think about what to do next. On the drive home, I realized it was actually better at this point if my sisters didn't know about me, because I could use this to bargain with her. She has something I want, and I have something she wants: she wants me to be a ghost, and I want to find my grandpa. And since her overriding concern was hiding me and my history from my sisters, I would tell her that I would not spill the beans to them if she would tell me who my father was.

Lillie had told me some years before that she didn't think Pat actually knew who my father was when she met him; a fact Pat would later confirm to Zippy.

I went home and started formulating exactly what I wanted to say to her. I wanted to talk to her in a way that was compassionate, but no-nonsense. I wanted her to understand absolutely that I meant what I was saying. I detested the feeling that I'd been pushed into a corner, and I regretted that being cornered made me feel like pushing *her* into a corner.

I slept on it.

The next morning I awoke and went to work. I mulled it over on the way into town, and realized this course of action might destroy any chance at a decent relationship with this woman, but the objective was finding my father, and—ultimately—my grandfather.

It was a Wednesday afternoon, and I called Pat Nail.

I wanted to avoid Zippy picking up the phone, which is why I called during the day—anticipating Zippy would be at work.

Pat answered. "Hello?"

"This is Rhonda Noonan, do you remember who I am from yesterday?" I said slowly.

"Yes."

"I know that you do not want my sisters to know about me."

"That's right."

"You and I both know that Robert Schultz is not my biological father...."

"Yes."

"So I will make you a deal...you have my word that I will never contact my sisters, as long as you are alive, if you will tell me the truth about my biological father. If I have not heard from you by Friday at noon, my first call will be to Zippy. You need to get a pen and paper. I'm going to give you my phone number..."

I told her my number and she repeated it back to me. I said "Now, you understand that I need to hear from you by Friday noon, and if you tell me the truth, you will not hear from me again."

"Yes," she replied.

"Bye."

"Bye."

When I got home that evening, the phone rang, and it was an unknown number to me. So I answered it.

"Hello?"

"Rhonda?"

"Yes."

"This is your sister Glenda."

"Your adoptive mom would help you if she could...if she had the authority. They are famous...kinda like the king or queen of England. They talk funny, like they are from England, with thick tongues. They are British. You have a brother. He had a stepfather. You will find that out. Your grandfather was at the level of a president."

———

*Lillie, 1998*

# 12

# "The end of the beginning"

I t was my half-sister Glenda on the phone.

"Well, I guess the cat's out of the bag," I said.

Glenda chuckled a bit. "Yes...Zippy picked up the phone in the other room when you called and heard the conversation. Probably wasn't the best thing to threaten Mother."

Clearly I had miscalculated about Zippy being at work. I agreed that it probably wasn't the best first impression for my half-sister to hear me blackmailing Pat. But I can't really imagine how any compassionate person wouldn't understand my situation. And both Glenda and Zippy were *very* compassionate.

"I wasn't threatening her, I was proposing a deal that would give us both what we wanted," I explained. "You have to understand that I have looked for this woman for more than twenty-eight years, and the idea that she doesn't feel like I deserve to know who I am...well, trust me, I won't stop until I find out."

And I wouldn't. Pat Nail could like it or not. At this point her desires were not at the top of my priority list. I had compassion for her situation but I was more than done with not having the truth about *me*. I wished the situation were different, but I didn't have options in it. Having a relationship with her looked increasingly unrealistic. That part of this "reunion" held little emotional consequence for me, really, at this point. The fact that she had refused to talk with me more than ten years earlier was not forgotten. She didn't want to see me and I didn't have to have a relationship with her. I needed information from her, but I didn't hold out much hope for that either, now.

Glenda and I talked about an hour and a half. She told me about her life and I told her about mine. We basically caught up—but it was an entire lifetime of catch-up. It felt really good, actually, to connect like that to someone I finally knew was genetic family—my first real biological connection. She was so warm, and compassionate, and genuinely interested and interesting.

She said Zippy had suspected that Pat had an out-of-wedlock child for many years, and that neither of them was the least bit surprised to hear this. It wasn't so much a discovery as a confirmation. They both wanted a chance to talk to Pat and see if they could get the entire story out of her, but Pat had already told Zippy that my dad's name was...Robert Mosier.

Huh? *Robert Mosier?* What happened to Gafford and Schultz? Who the hell was Robert Mosier?

She didn't even know how to spell his name. She knew very little about him. She said he moved to Texas from Oklahoma City; that he was "a used car salesman."

*Hmmm,* I thought; *Rhonda Gafford/Noonan/ Schultz/ Mosier...*wonder who's next? I couldn't imagine that the FBI would have concerned themselves with a used car salesman.

Glenda and I talked and talked and talked. She was so reassuring. She explained how Zippy had listened to my conversation with Pat, and she laughed and said "You'd never have gotten anywhere trying to blackmail mom, because she is so stubborn, she would've just dug in deeper." But I explained that I felt it was my only option. She said not to worry, that she and Zippy didn't hold any grudges, and that they wanted to meet me.

I told them I felt likewise about them, and they let me know that Pat, on the other hand, wanted nothing more to do with me. She had commented to Zippy that I was "nothing but trouble."

Can you imagine? This woman gave birth to me, then gave me up for adoption—during which I was stripped of my identity and emotionally traumatized. And, now, after half a lifetime, I finally knocked on her door, so that she had to actually look me in the face and speak to me for the first time since I was an infant—and I'm "nothing but trouble"? It wobbles the mind. I told myself that I should feel hurt by her comment. Wouldn't that be the normal response? But it was hard to access my emotions concerning this woman. It just made me even more determined that her attitude would not derail my efforts.

Pat Nail aside, I was overjoyed by the anticipation of meeting my sisters face-to-face. We set up a time the following Saturday to see each other.

I called Mom and told her I had found my birthmother. She was happy for me, but ambivalent. She was glad I had found what I was looking for, but worried how I would be treated by my long-lost genetic relatives, and afraid they might not treat her well, either. Little did I know that Pat had no intention of seeing me at all, whether my sisters saw me or not.

The following Saturday, I loaded up all my paperwork: my court documents, birth certificate, court orders, thirty years of documents pertaining to the search—an entire box—and drove back to Purcell, Oklahoma.

Glenda was there waiting for me when I arrived at her home. She phoned Zippy, who then came right over. They looked just like their dad, they had reported, and I looked a great deal like my birthmother. In fact the very second each one of them laid eyes one me, there was zero doubt about my relationship to Pat Nail. They had been staring at her face all their lives, and her features registered strongly enough in my face that they stared at me quite a long time, astonished at the resemblance.

Pat, however, was not going to see me. She stayed two doors down at Zippy's house, and we stayed at Glenda's.

Glenda made bacon and tomato sandwiches which she served with potato chips and iced tea. We sat down at the table in the kitchen and started poring over every document. They shared memories about their childhoods with Pat, putting the pieces together and collectively reassembling a history that had been shrouded in Pat's attempts to erase my origins. They looked through the court records and discussed them with each other. I related the story of all my legal trials, and the hundreds of dead ends, and the decades of searching and phony names.

Speaking of phony names, I wondered, how did "Irene Pruitt" become "Pat Nail" anyway?

"Well," Glenda said, "it just kinda happened…she remarried a Nail. And 'Pat' was a nickname at first, that ended up sticking." The better, I thought, to help her hide and avoid discovery.

They told me that their dad had been killed in a car wreck, and in a really bizarre turn, they explained that the man on my birth certificate was actually their uncle—my mom's brother-in-law. And, he didn't even live in Oklahoma, he lived in Colorado.

Wow. How bizarre.

They told me how odd it was—the period of time right before and right after my birth, during which they moved to Shawnee. Pat had sent them away before she had me, and they didn't see her for another month after I was born. No one really knew where she was or what she was doing. At that time, Pat told Glenda she was "having an operation."

According to my sisters, their mother had never been overt with displays of physical affection when they were young. But when she returned from having me (and turning me over to the state), she sat my youngest sister, Caroline in her lap, and tearfully explained how much she loved her, and told them all they were her sweet babies. Zippy and Glenda found that odd—coming from a woman who had seldom been explicitly emotional.

They talked about how secretive Pat had always been about her life, even about her comings and goings. When she left the house, no one asked where she went. They "just knew," according to Glenda, that "you didn't ask Mother where she was going."

Apparently she would often go out dancing, especially at a club in Oklahoma City called Kochi's. That was one of the places where the rich and famous hung out. They remembered hearing that Johnny Cash had been there one night. Pat also frequented the Officers' Club at Tinker Air Force Base. Those were the "two places you went out to dance and socialize," according to my sisters. She was known to be a regular character in that social scene, along with a good girl friend of hers. Zippy commented that she never felt like her mother lacked for a social life; that she always had dates and enjoyed going out.

While Pat was pregnant with me, she sent two of my sisters to visit relatives in Texas. She told the other two that they were going to summer camp, but they actually went to stay with a foster family. I found that interesting. Who could have authorized it? DHS wasn't in the habit of sending siblings off to foster families if their mom was having a baby. The family had abruptly moved from Oklahoma City to Shawnee during the pregnancy, and my sisters remembered several instances in which men would show up at their Shawnee home—men they had not seen before and did not know. Pat was very secretive and tried to hide this from them.

Times had been hard for them financially. They made the move with zero money, and stayed in Shawnee for about four months—just long enough for Pat to have me. Zippy and Glenda reported they saw "at least two different men" come to the door, and there was a hand-off of some money on one occasion. Another time, when Zippy happened to have stayed home sick from school, Pat answered a knock and said, "My daughter's home," then quickly shut the door without another word to the caller.

Zippy knew what Bob Mosier looked like. They had seen him and knew it wasn't Mosier that came by on that occasion. Glenda saw another tall man—elegant looking, curly dark hair, nice suit—come around a time or two. At this time Zippy was fourteen years old and Glenda was twelve.

We talked and bonded for almost five hours. There were so many details, and more questions than answers by the end of the afternoon. When I showed them all the documents signed by Pat, Zippy said, "Well, that's mother's signature. No doubt about that." There were places she signed "Irene Pruitt," and others "Irene Pruitt Gafford," but the girls confirmed that they were all her handwriting.

We were glued to each other's biographical tales that afternoon, even as the sun sank, casting long shadows across the yard. I was soaking up their whole history and they were soaking up mine. But I was still on a mission—to find my birthfather and grandfather.

I needed help from my sisters. I needed them to tell me everything they knew, so I could find what I was looking for. Sadly, Pat was not in good health. I knew her time was limited, and I knew if she was going to talk about this, she would talk to one of my sisters, so I was hoping and praying for their assistance to help me solve the mystery.

I had two sisters I still hadn't met. Glenda and Zippy called Caroline and Lenore.

I stopped in Eufaula to see Caroline. She met me at the door, and appeared to be quite overwhelmed by the entire situation. She told me that she couldn't believe she had missed all those years with me, and was so glad to finally meet me. She hugged me and cried. I told her she would never be without me again and that I was thrilled to meet her, too.

I sat down at the kitchen table and showed her some of the documents. "I just want you to know that I am who I say

I am." Pat had never denied me, but I wanted her to see the evidence for herself.

Not that it was necessary. One look at my face made that truth incontrovertible to anyone who knew Pat Nail's visage very well. Still I went through the documents, and told Caroline I was looking for my biological father. I assured her that it was never my intention to impose myself on Pat or cause her any problems. My sisters were unaware that DHS had spoken to Pat in 1998 and that she had refused to see me. I told her that there was a lot of mystery around my birth—the FBI story, the bizarre happenings, etc.—and that my grandmother had been told my family was famous.

Caroline's husband was sitting on the couch, openly expressing his disbelief the entire time I was relaying my story. He kept breaking in with, "Oh, that's ridiculous. There's no way."

I acknowledged his comments by politely admitting that I was sure it was all a shock and made for quite a story, but it had happened just as I was telling it. Addressing Caroline directly, I kept telling the story, occasionally looking his way as if to say, "I'm not talking to you!"

"Oh well, that's just ridiculous!" he said again. I cut my stay short, told Caroline I was pleased to meet her, and departed. I have not seen or talked to her since.

It was clear that Lenore had a brazen streak. She was very bold and outspoken—the kind of person who would be the foreman on any jury. She had an almost dauntingly frank personality. She had invited me to her house in Moore for lunch. During our meeting she asked, "So, you think there's something more to this adoption thing?"

"Yes," I answered.

"Okay, well, if Mom will tell anyone she'll tell me."

I was impressed by her interest and helpful response and liked her immediately.

I was dying to know the story. I couldn't believe I had waited all these years and gone through all I had, tracked her down and eventually met her—only for her to say *nothing*. Surely she would weigh the fact of passing time, recognize that it would be okay now, and tell the story of the events surrounding my birth.

Almost a week passed, and Lenore called to say, "Rhonda, Mother doesn't want to talk about it, and I can tell you that I will never bring it up to her again."

Lenore had pushed Pat to open up, and apparently Pat broke down sobbing and crying. Lenore felt it was just too upsetting to ever broach the subject again.

But Lenore's tone was almost accusatory—as if I had forced her to approach Pat. I was happy she'd offered to get the story, but I hadn't insisted on it. In fact, I never even asked her to talk to Pat. She was the self-appointed investigator. My half-sister's position quickly became: "My mom is very elderly and probably doesn't remember. It will not be discussed with her again."

I made it pretty clear to Lenore that I didn't accept her take on things. Of *course* she remembered. And it was almost an outrage for anyone (especially another woman) to pretend Pat would've just "forgotten" that. That was nonsense. I knew if there was even one functional neuron left in Pat Nail's brain—and there clearly was—she remembered with crystal clarity exactly who my father was. I was incensed at the frivolousness and ridiculousness of the very suggestion that she could possibly forget. But they stuck to it. If Pat persisted with tears any time it was mentioned, she could avoid all of it.

So everyone was at an impasse.

Zippy did ask Pat about Robert Schultz. Pat replied, "That never happened."

Zippy finally (and quite rightfully) countered with, "Mother, it happened. Rhonda met the man. She *met* him mother!"

Confronted with the reality that Zippy and Glenda knew I didn't invent Robert Schultz—that I had actually met him—Pat changed her tone. She flippantly replied, "I knew she would never get anywhere with him." That was a pivotal moment for Zippy, as she then knew Pat had not told the truth about Schultz.

I was blown away by this woman's stubbornness and stonewalling. I thought finding my genetic family would be a "checkmate" of sorts, but it had ended up raising a lot more questions than it answered.

I found them. Everything was supposed to be resolved now, right? But nothing was resolved. Everyone had met everyone, and still *nothing* was settled.

I was at my desk at work, depressed, frustrated and without any idea of how to proceed. I knew Pat Nail wasn't going to share anything. I was growing increasingly anxious, realizing that she was dying, that they were *all* dying—everyone tied to my story. *They'll all soon be dead,* I thought, *and the trail will go cold. It's taking me too long!*

As had been the case many times over the past twenty-five years, I longed to talk to Lillie. I decided to give Monica a call and request some time. Monica left a message that she could phone me the following evening and give me a reading. It would be the perfect opportunity for Denna and Harriet to hear a reading for themselves, as well as help me sort through any clues Monica might offer. I had heard the "story" so many times that someone else's take on it might be valuable. I called Denna.

At seven o'clock the three of us gathered around the cell phone. Monica asked what was going on, and I told her that I had found my birthmother, but that she refused to divulge anything to me, and I was counting on the help of my sisters.

She interrupted me: "Lillie says you are following trails that are far from the center...your grandfather was the level of a president. Your sisters are not going to be able to help you. Lillie is saying, your father is British. He died in 1968."

Lillie kept the information flowing, as though there was so much to say she didn't know what to share next. "Your angels are jumping up and down," she said. "Would you like to know why you have the name you have?" I said of course I would. "There is a valley...the Rhonda Valley, and there is a connection with your family. It is spelled with two D's or two N's, instead of one."

Harriet began combing the Internet. She called from the other room, "There is a valley in the extreme southeastern part of Wales. It is called the Rhondda...spelled with two D's...." It was, she read, a coal mining area. I couldn't imagine what this had to do with me.

Lillie continued to direct Monica. "She is saying 'Bess is holding you, Bess is holding you.' She is asking about September and saying 'two months...there was a transition at two months...he was there when they gave you to someone'...now Lillie is telling me that 'he was wearing the ring during the exchange.' What is two months...what does two months mean?" I replied that it was two months after I was born on July 8. Monica went on, "At two months there was an exchange...he was wearing the ring. I'm going to describe it to you. She is showing it to me. It is kind of square, and gold in color. There is a black background with a 'C' in the middle. Lillie says this is a big clue."

Suddenly Monica took off on something else: "There is a piece of wood. It is rectangular and has an AAA or ALA on it, with H Heflin," which she spelled out to me. "I don't know why that matters but that's what Lillie's telling me."

Just a couple of minutes later, Harriet announced, "Oh, my gosh, I found it. It's a desk and it has those names on it. Come look." She explained that she was looking on President Truman's Library website. Sure enough, she had a picture of the exact desktop being described, with the "H Heflin" carved into it and "ALA" below that. Above that name, in the middle of the desktop, was "Truman, Mo." The desk had been used by a senator (Heflin) from Alabama, and then by Harry Truman, while they were in the senate. It was unbelievable that Harriet found it, almost immediately after Lillie passed the information to Monica.

It was a surreal and amazing experience. Lillie was directive and confident. Why was she talking about Truman? What part did he play in all this, if anything?

Monica talked about Lillie's excitement and devotion to this search and her support for me. She said, "You're very close now." But these clues only made me feel farther away. It was exciting to have the Internet pull some pieces together, but the pieces were so confusing, and there was nothing yet to unify them into a story...*my* story.

*Okay,* I told myself after the call had ended and Denna and Harriet had gone home. *Go back to the beginning and look at it all. Be methodical. Look at the obvious and question everything. Again.* I replayed all that I had done...the people I had talked to, the situations I had explored. What else could I do now? There *had* to be something.

Then I had a thought about how people love to talk. And the fact that the people who were actually involved in all this may be dead or dying, but their children were probably around; people who might have heard or seen something. I made a list of all of the names in all my files and records, and then proceeded to identify and locate any and all of their descendants. This brought me back to the scene of the mystery: the Tonkawa families, Cookson, Yocum, and Dixon, as well as Governor Gary.

I phoned my Mom....

"A judge will give you the records. He'll ask you why you want them and you'll say because you want to know your blood. You will want a test. The FBI can work on it and uncover who you are, have been, and were at birth."

———

*Lillie, 1997*

# 13

# "Blood, toil, tears and sweat"

"Hi, Mom. I need your help, please. Can you tell me which of the following people had kids, and what their names are, and maybe where I can find them?" She said she would be more than happy to share everything she could remember. I asked about Ralph Cookson. "Yes, he had a daughter named Cathy...and I think I can get her number for you."

She did, and I called Cathy Cookson. No one ever knew what Ralph Cookson did, because he worked around so many powerful people, but had no identifiable job description. The word on the street was that he was a hit man. Now his daughter was telling me he had been an "executive assistant" to Governor Gary. (I later spoke with a state historian in Oklahoma City who said Cookson was not part of Raymond Gary's administration in any formal, documented role—and certainly not his executive assistant.) Cathy also confirmed that her dad had "business interests" with Lloyd Rader, the Director of Social Services.

My next name for Mom had been Mrs. Roy Gardener. She was the caseworker that called on my parents and grandparents in preparation for my adoption. My magical searcher friend Linda Colvard had document upon document about Mrs. Gardener, who had been a leader in the state Human Services division and been well respected among her peers.

She gave me the address and phone number of Gardener's

son—her only living child, as her daughter had contracted terminal cancer and died two years earlier...just a year after Gardener herself.

I called and talked to the son, who lived in Kentucky. He said his mother had been very discreet and never spoke about any of her cases. *Shocker,* I thought. The "system" had created these "sacred record-keepers." They were devoted to inhuman, life-destroying secrets. The abolishment of truth. That was a dead end.

Mom had said Sam Dixon, the Ford dealer, had two sons, Brad and Bert. A friend of mine was friends with both of them. She asked Brad if he would be willing to talk to me and gave him my number. The next day he called, and I asked if he'd be willing to sit down with me. He agreed.

I had never laid eyes on him before. But this was a big day. We went to the Starbucks on Yale and sat outside. It was a really pretty day. I introduced myself and said, "I bet you're curious as to why I called you."

He chuckled, and said, "Well, yes, I am."

Brad was a kind and wise man. I told him I was adopted, and that there was a series of very strange events surrounding my adoption: the tapping of my parents' phone, the FBI showing up in Tonkawa, and the strange way in which I was handed off to them at the hotel. I told him that I believed the group of men his dad ran around with had something to do with me being placed with the Noonans, and I was trying to put the pieces together. I said, "I'm going to give you some names, and please give me any info about your dad's relationships with them if that's okay." Brad agreed. I started with Ralph Cookson. "Oh yes, Dad knew Ralph Cookson."

"Everett and Roy Yocum?"

"Yes, he knew both of them."

Then, it got interesting.

"Robert Mosier?" I asked. And I will never forget his response. He tipped backwards in his chair a little bit, and paused, and said, "Do you mean R.E. Bob Mosier?"

"Yeah."

"Oh yes, Dad knew him well. I don't know the extent of their dealings, but yes, he has been to our house and dad certainly knew him. Bob Mosier was a car dealer."

I immediately knew that I had established the link from Oklahoma City to Tonkawa, because Robert Mosier had known my birthmother. She had claimed he was my father.

So R.E. Bob Mosier could have easily passed information around in that circle of friends...Cookson, Harold, Dixon, Rader, Gary, *Mosier and Pat Nail*... the connections were clear now. I was thrilled and intrigued. I went on and told Brad a good deal of the story. He was very interested and very helpful. But he didn't know anyone, directly associated with his father, who was high-profile enough to do the things I described. Still, he said he would be happy to help in any way he could.

I knew my Grandfather Harold had gone to Ralph Cookson, soliciting his help in finding a baby for my parents. And Cookson was involved on a daily basis with both the governor and with Lloyd Rader—as well as Sam Dixon and Robert Mosier. Wow. Mosier would've known of the pregnancy. And because Mosier was a business associate of Cookson and Dixon and Rader, they would have all been aware of the fact that Howard Harold's daughter wanted a baby. But *whose* baby was I?

Locating and talking to Brad Dixon had proved valuable indeed. Next would be Raymond Gary. Once again I enlisted the help of Linda Colvard to see if he had any children. She located one Mona May Waymire, who was Gary's daughter.

Mona was very nice. I spoke to her twice. The first time she said she couldn't think of a thing that would be of help and certainly was not aware of any potentially high-profile adoption.

I called her back a few days later, and asked her a little differently: "Can you tell me if there was anyone at the level of a president that your dad had anything to do with when he was governor?"

"No." She couldn't think of anyone. The closest she could imagine was Governor Harriman. "But he wouldn't have needed any favors from my dad." I asked if she knew if Harriman was ever in Oklahoma City, but she had no knowledge of that.

I also told Mona May that the FBI fellow I had talked to at the Pentagon told me that the only way the Bureau would be involved in an adoption was if the parent of the child were a foreign dignitary or diplomat. I explained that the FBI had been in Tonkawa asking questions around the time of my birth. She said she couldn't think of anyone at that level that her father was involved with—again, except for Averell Harriman.

I thanked her for her willingness to talk to me and focused on Harriman. Who was he?

I immediately sat down with Google, and discovered that he had been ambassador to Britain and governor of New York. I compared all that I knew from my limited DHS information and what Lillie had told me, and Harriman didn't fit. Still I read on...he had an affair with the wife of Randolph Churchill, Winston Churchill's son, and later married her.

The Churchills? I sat up straight in my chair. Now I'd hit something.

I read about Harriman's long relationship with the Churchills. Randolph worked as a political reporter, and had come to America to cover the presidential primaries—in which Harriman was a candidate for the Democratic nomination.

My head was swimming. All of the things Lillie had told me about my biological father—about his relationship with his father, about his alcoholism, the fact that he had died in 1968, that he was British...everything she had said about my grandfather, and his place in history...suddenly, startlingly, *fit*.

I almost didn't dare to draw the conclusion that was now pressing on me. First I decided to go back to some of the other clues Lillie had given me. I looked up the Rhondda Valley. And I found Winston Churchill.

In 1910, when he was Home Secretary, a group of miners in the Rhondda began the Tonypandy Riot. The Chief Constable of the area requested that troops be sent in to stop the rioting. Although they had been ordered deployed, and were en route, Winston allowed them to travel only as far as Swindon and Cardiff, then blocked the deployment. He came under criticism all the same, and was blamed for ordering troops to attack. This rumor persists to this day and caused his reputation damage.

My first inclination was to sign up for a psychological evaluation...surely I must be insane. Could this be true? Winston Churchill...my grandfather?

Churchill descended from nobility, for heaven's sake. John Churchill was the first Duke of Marlborough, given the title in 1702 by Queen Anne. Because he had no surviving sons, the title moved forward when Lady Anne Churchill married Charles Spencer, thus creating the Spencer-Churchill surname.

Over time, many family members chose to use only the Churchill name. The 9th Duke of Marlborough, Charles Richard Spencer-Churchill, was Winston Churchill's first cousin. Interestingly, Charles married two American women in his life: Consuelo Vanderbilt and Gladys Marie Deacon. When he divorced Consuelo in 1921, the Vanderbilt dowry was used to restore Blenheim Palace, the ancestral home of the Dukes of Marlborough and the birthplace of Winston Churchill.

The idea that this grand pageant of ancestry could in fact be mine was almost disorienting.

To be certain of it, I had to place Randolph Churchill in Oklahoma at the time of my conception; something I suspected would not be easy.

As I investigated further, I learned that some historians believe Sir Winston himself was likely illegitimate. I knew he had an American mother and a detached and distant relationship with his father. He certainly could have felt compassion for my parallel plight.

But at the same time I was reading all these things, I couldn't get my mind around the possibility that a man of such historical significance could be the man I had been searching for these thirty years. It blew my mind to contemplate the possibility that Winston Churchill could be my grandfather.

I sat and looked at photos of Randolph, and the most shocking one of all was the only close-up of his teeth; I thought, oh my gosh—there are *my* teeth. Prior to having my teeth capped and fixed, they were identical to his.

I noticed his legs, the way he stood, even the way he walked. I realized I had the same gait. Of course, internally, I wasn't convinced. I thought it must all be an amazing coincidence...and just as quickly dealt with the reality that I don't believe in coincidences.

And as if to confirm this, I found a video of Randolph's appearance on a 1956 TV show called *What's My Line*. There is a shot of his hand in which he appears to sport a signet ring with a "C" and dark background—exactly like the ring Lillie described being worn by the man present as I was handed over to the state at two months old. Bingo! I searched to establish a time frame for the taping of the show. It aired in February 1956 but the recording date eluded me.

I asked myself, how on earth could Randolph Churchill be responsible for me? What would he have been doing in Oklahoma?

The references to President Truman and his wife, Bess, were equally perplexing. Not having information from my birthmother about the events immediately following my delivery, it was impossible to know how the former president might have assisted with the adoption. Clearly Truman was a friend of the Churchills, and the state of Missouri had been mentioned in readings before.

All of this seemed stranger than fiction. You just couldn't make it up.

The more carefully I studied Averell Harriman, the more I realized that his relationship with Raymond Gary had been a close one, politically. The Democrats were looking at Gary as a possible vice-presidential candidate should Harriman win the nomination. And as I researched newspaper articles I learned that Gary had traveled to New York City to meet Harriman just prior to the premier of the musical *Oklahoma*. They took publicity photos for the play.

Lillie had always talked about my grandpa being British and at "the level of a president." She knew that my grandfather and father were already deceased; that my father had a tumultuous relationship with his father, and that my mother would have been way below his social class. She said my family was steeped in history, and that my "grandfather would be in history books." She had talked about race horses and alcoholism, and....

My mind was swimming. I contemplated my common sense...or lack thereof. How could this be?

It wasn't long after this that I learned my mom wanted to call and talk to my birthmother. She asked if I was okay with it. I thought it would be interesting to hear what Pat might say but doubted sincerely that she would talk to Mom at all. In fact the request never even reached her. I dialed the phone for Mom, and Zippy answered. I told her my mom wanted to talk to Pat. Zippy explained there was "no way," and that was the end of that.

Mom was disappointed, saying she only wanted to thank Pat for "giving me such a wonderful child." I, on the other hand, was relieved that I didn't have to worry about Mom's feelings being hurt. Knowing where Pat stood, it didn't seem a good idea for them to speak. What a strange collision of maternal characters that might have been: one woman who had been swimming in kids and had abdicated her role as mother; another who had been childless, and climbed mountains to secure her role as mother.

We hung up the phone and slid back into our daily routines.

Weeks turned into months, and one day Zippy said: "Let's have you come down for lunch—with Mother. I'll ask Lenore and Glenda to join us."

So we planned a date for the four of us and Pat. I drove to Zippy's, walked in, and sat down at the table. There we were for the first time since my "blackmail" attempt.

During the entire two hours we were there, Pat Nail spoke no more than twice. She sat at one end of the table, and I sat to one side. Every time I would look at my sisters, in my peripheral vision I could see her watching me. But not one single time did she look me in the eye when I looked at her. Can you imagine?

I said one thing to her during the entire meeting, and she responded with a single sentence. And at another point she spoke another sentence—she told Zippy to turn the fan off because she didn't want it blowing on her food when we ate. It was fascinating in that I have never, in my life, been comfortable eating food under a blowing ceiling fan. I have been known by friends to get up and turn off a fan when food was served.

The lunch was delicious, but the event was uncomfortable. When we were leaving, Pat clearly avoided making any move in my direction as I was hugging my sisters. She might have succeeded if not for Zippy saying, "Mom get over here, and give her a hug."

Pat obeyed. I had zero desire to hug someone who clearly did not want to hug me, but I decided to go with the flow, then leave as fast as possible without making anyone feel uncomfortable or awkward. She hugged me and walked away.

It had become more than clear at this point that Pat was never going to be cool with me. Zippy had told me she thought Pat might actually try to normalize things between us. I took that to mean that she would build a façade of social responsibility and acceptability, and even if not genuine, keep up some appearances. But after that day, I knew it would never happen. She told Zippy, "Now, maybe she will go away." I never saw Pat again.

I felt compassion for my birthmother and was acutely aware of the fact that she had never wanted to deal with me; that I had pushed this nasty secret on her. But I never understood her position, and she never shed any light on it. How could a mother not want to see her child? My sisters had embraced me; I was thankful for that. Surely that had been reassuring to Pat. Unfortunately, she wasn't letting anyone in on what had actually happened to her all those years ago.

I believed she had been threatened and treated badly; probably she was told very clearly what she was to do with me. It might well have been a horrifying time for her. Something made her see me as a problem all those years later. Pat had told DHS that she felt no affection for my father; that she had not known him. My sisters had shared with me that, despite the fact that it was two years after my birth that Pat dated Robert Mosier, she had cared a great deal for him. If he had been my father, she would not have spoken so negatively about him. None of it made any sense!

Clearly it had not been an easy situation for her. She seemed to be harboring real anger about the circumstances surrounding my birth; I simply could not comprehend why that anger was directed towards *me*. Was the whole Robert Schultz charade forced on her? Perhaps the clairvoyant I had consulted was correct. Maybe she was threatened in ways I cannot imagine. Perhaps she believed silence was necessary to protect her family from harm. I did not appreciate her silence but I tried to understand it.

My birthmother would dislike me to her grave, and there would never be a blasted thing I could do about any of it. As I have always believed that things happen the way they are supposed to, I tried to simply accept what was.

I was talking to Zippy one day, and she told me that Lenore had read an article in the *Oklahoman* which mentioned something about Lloyd Rader having kept daily logs and records which were maintained at the University of Central Oklahoma. Zippy thought it would be wise to check there for anything that might remotely relate to my adoption. So I investigated.

I contacted a woman at UCO who said some of the records were publicly available and some weren't, and I would just have to show up and discuss all that in person. So, I went down there and was given piles and boxes of stuff. I was buried in materials—thousands of pages. I very quickly realized there was vastly more there than I could get through in a millennium. Only a small amount of the data was catalogued chronologically. I looked for 1955 and 1956, but there was nothing specific about adoptions—*anyone's* adoption.

It had been another good idea, and I'm glad I made the effort, but it yielded nothing. I had to find someone else directly related to my history.

Of course, always in the back of my mind was Randolph Churchill and any possibility that he was in Oklahoma City.

"You are going to go to England.
An older woman could tell you a lot
you'd like to know. One of them will
step forward and want to help. They will
want to do the right thing. They would
see you but feel guilty. Excuses, excuses…
They will say they didn't know
where you were."

———

*Lillie, 1997*

# 14

# "Never, never, never, never give in"

I n 2006 I contacted Chris Wright, the fellow in charge of the history archives at Tinker Air Force Base. He did some research for me into the year 1955. I told him to look around September and October of that year.

We learned that the club didn't have a sign-in register. They did host a lot of musical events. He told me about all the swing bands they had booked. Back in the 1950s, a lot of these bands had mob ties. The mob made their bookings and took a percentage of their earnings.

I kept researching for any record of Randolph Churchill coming to Oklahoma, and in the process I read an account of a trip Raymond Gary made back to Oklahoma from New York City, after a meeting with Harriman. During the trip the plane carrying Gary and his brother lost an engine and made an emergency landing in Oklahoma City.

I tried to find out if Churchill was also a passenger that night. I located the daughter of the plane's pilot, who was a decorated World War II fighter pilot. She was very kind and offered to go through her documents to look for mention of Randolph Churchill. She had "fourteen boxes full of stuff," but never found any passenger manifest from that night.

I read many accounts of Raymond Gary and Harriman being in contact during that time, and Harriman had planned to come to Oklahoma on a couple of occasions. But did it happen, and did his friend Randolph come with him?

I combed back through every page in my file, over and over and over. Surely these piles of paperwork, amassed over almost three decades, would yield something I hadn't seen before. I reread every record for the hundredth, no, thousandth time...went back over the doctor's first comments about me—when they called me "Baby Kim"—through how he would see me again for more psychological testing when I was four months old. And how he CC'd Polly Hunt.

Hmm. Perhaps Polly Hunt was still alive and would mercifully provide some shreds of information surrounding the events. I looked in the phone book again, and there she was: Polly Hunt. I called, but there was no answer.

Denna and I decided to drive to her last known address and talk to any neighbor I could find. A woman in the complex knew Polly and told us she had moved to an assisted living facility outside Edmond. We immediately headed that way. Finding it easily, I approached the desk and signed in. A nurse inquired as to what I needed and I told her I would like to visit with Polly Hunt.

"Yes ma'am, she's in room 417."

I found her room, and saw her. She was very frail, and marked by the solemnity of a person winding up her time on earth. She was in a wheelchair and had an oxygen tank in tow wherever she went. I think she was ninety-four when I first visited her. I introduced myself, and told her that I was an adoptee.

"One of mine?" she asked.

I told her that she worked on my case in the mid-fifties. We chatted about how she had been, and she started talking about some of her cases. She said, "I always hoped I did the right thing by the children...I always worried about that."

I assured her she had done right by me. "I had a wonderful home and great family."

I was very pleased that she was talking shop—because if she would talk about other cases, perhaps we could shift into talking about mine. The nurse broke in to announce that Polly's lunch was ready. I told her I would sit with her while she ate.

She finished lunch, and I asked if we might go somewhere quiet to talk. "Yes, the TV room," she suggested.

"You were one of my kids," she said when we settled in there.

"That's right. I was one of your kids." I didn't know how to go about asking what I wanted to know. Inside, I felt like pleading with her: *Please, please tell me the truth.* If she only knew what I'd been through and how important this was to me, she'd help me. I wanted her to know that there was no one else who could tell me for sure. The importance of the moment was suffocating me. I didn't know what to do. I kept thinking: *The truth...just tell the truth.* So I just laid it out.

"Polly, I want to know if you can tell me anything about my dad. I recently found and met my birthmother, but there's all kinds of confusion about who my dad is, and I'm trying to piece together the whole story. My mom and dad were Jim and Jean-lee Noonan from Tonkawa, Oklahoma. Irene Gafford was my birthmother. She was a hairdresser...one of the DHS workers was her friend. Was that you? There was a big cover-up with the FBI and moving the family to Shawnee. That baby was me."

Polly looked down and with grave seriousness said, "Ol' Rader didn't scare easily, but Churchill scared him to death."

I thought my heart had stopped beating. I hadn't dared to believe, but could this really be? I wanted to hug her, scream out loud, jump up and down.

"Did you just say 'Churchill'...as in Randolph Churchill?"

"You shouldn't be talking about this," Polly said, and a look of fear came over her face. "You mustn't tell anyone about this. Somebody's liable to get hurt. Don't talk about it."

"No we're safe. You're safe. Everything's okay, because all those people are gone. They've passed away. Tell me what happened Polly...you saw him?"

"Lloyd Rader called me into his office. I thought I was in trouble...big trouble. I was worried. There was a meeting. But I wasn't in trouble. There were papers on the table. Churchill came in, tipped his hat to us and put it on the table. He was there to sign. They were talking about you." I told her I had suspected this.

"Polly, are you sure you remember this right?"

"I wouldn't have let myself forget that," she replied softly. "You shouldn't be talking about this." She looked away, as though finished with the conversation.

I thanked her—profusely. She replied, "Meeting Churchill was like meeting Moses."

I was so shocked by what she was telling me, and knew I wanted a witness to everything. I thought no one would believe it. Denna was out in the parking lot and I did not want to interrupt this conversation. I hollered out the door at an aide who was passing, named Shari Wilkins.

Shari came over, and I said, "Please, I need a witness to what Polly is telling me, can you please listen?"

She said, "Yes. Ms. Polly used to work with kids."

I replied, "I know, I'm one of them," and asked Polly to please tell me about the meeting again.

Polly retold the story and Shari nodded her head that she had heard. Polly cautioned her, "You must not tell anybody about this. You have to keep it secret. It's not good, not good... you can't talk about it. It's too dangerous. You'll get in trouble."

Again, I tried to reassure her, "Polly, everybody's dead. Nobody's going to get in trouble. Everyone's dead that had anything to do with it except you and my birthmother."

She asked if my birthmother had talked to me about it, and I told her no, which is why I had come to her about it. That was basically the end of the discussion.

I gathered my things, and I walked out of that facility singing the Hallelujah chorus. I could now place Randolph

Churchill in the middle of my case!

I planned to come back and visit Polly in a few days. I wanted not only to have a witness, but a written document of what she said. I also hoped for more details to emerge as her aging mind replayed the event.

In the car on the way home I began writing down her statements as I told Denna what had transpired. My plan was to type up a transcript of the conversation as well as a statement as to my identity, and take it back for Polly to verify. I thought it might prove helpful as I continued to move forward.

The following week I made the trip to Edmond again. "Polly I would like you to read this." I said. But she had lost a lot of her eyesight in her nineties, so she asked me to read it to her.

I asked another of the aides to come over to the table, then asked Polly if she was okay with someone else listening in. She nodded, so I started reading: "I, Polly Hunt, recall a meeting with Lloyd Rader, myself, and Randolph Churchill, in which Randolph's affair with Rhonda Noonan's birthmother, Irene Pruitt-Gafford was discussed. This affair resulted in her pregnancy with Rhonda. This meeting was held in Oklahoma City—"

I got that far into the story, then noticed tears streaming down her face. "Polly, what's wrong?"

"I don't want you to read anymore. I don't want her to hear it," she said, looking over at the aide. "You'll be dodging bullets like I am," she said, then resumed sobbing. "You have to stop."

Dodging bullets? Holy cow...was she serious? Were the threats that severe? Did that explain Pat's response to me showing up?

"I'm not going to let anything bad happen to you," I assured her, and asked if the aide could read the statement I'd written. She agreed to that.

She finished reading it, and then Polly and I read it by ourselves. I wanted to make sure that it was correct and that Polly agreed. I asked the girl if she would sign off on what she had heard. She stated she would, then asked, "You're related to Winston Churchill?"

"Yes, can you believe that?"

Polly chuckled and said, "Who would've ever thought I would meet a Churchill?"

Finally I had a witness, and a witness to my witness, and a signed witness statement! And mountains of other circumstantial evidence to back up the direct evidence.

I also learned that while my paperwork showed Polly as the "caseworker," she actually outranked the directors of all the other departments at DHS as Rader's assistant. And not only was Polly operating in a position of power higher than what anyone knew, I also discovered that Bonnie Walton—my oldest sworn nemesis—was actually Lloyd Rader's niece.

Wow, it just kept getting more and more interesting by the day!

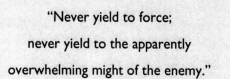

"Never yield to force;

never yield to the apparently

overwhelming might of the enemy."

——

*Winston Churchill*

# *"The problems of victory"*

On Thanksgiving, I called my sister Zippy and said: "It's Randolph Churchill."

Zippy knew exactly what I meant. She looked him up on the web, and asked my birthmother, "Is her father Randolph Churchill?"

"No, don't be ridiculous," answered Pat Nail.

"Mom, Rhonda knows! The DHS worker told her."

Silence.

There was nothing but silence from Pat Nail. Her entire life had been a symphony of silence. Soon, her health started to deteriorate, and as she went downhill my sisters tended to her, so that I had little communication with them. Pat made no mention of me. Period. She was hospitalized for pneumonia, but the doctors discovered lung cancer.

Now that Polly had confirmed Randolph Churchill, I talked to DNA services about what it would take to prove this relationship beyond any doubt. I consulted a company called Cellmark Orchid, and they said that because of the nature of half sibling tests, they would need DNA from my birthmother as part of a rule-out process. I asked Zippy to get some DNA from Pat the next time she was in the hospital. Zippy collected and saved some blood-stained cotton balls, and gave them to me. Thank God for Zippy, or I wouldn't have my maternal DNA blood sample.

One December morning, I decided to call Lenore and see

how she was. She informed me that "our mother" had died an hour before I called. I couldn't help wondering when I would have heard that news, had I not made that call. It was just a "coincidence" that I phoned when I did. Being adopted is so bizarre at times. What's the proper etiquette for one's birthmother dying? She didn't like me but I like my sisters, and… and, well it is what it is. Isn't it?

I wasn't invited to the funeral. Nor was anything mentioned about it to me.

Can you imagine how strange that was? I imagined it was due to the fact that the "camp" was divided, with Zippy and Glenda being sensitive to my cause and the other two sisters thinking I was crazy, and a stress to Pat.

I went to visit Lenore shortly afterward. Zippy joined us there. Lenore pulled out a tape of the funeral for me to watch. Not because I asked to see it, or even wanted to see it, but, I suspected, because she wanted me to feel included somehow. Who cares about a funeral that you weren't invited to? That sort of misses the whole point of a funeral. They're for the living—the family—and I missed it.

This was just one more bizarro-land event I endured on the subject of Pat Nail. Talk about feeling a-d-o-p-t-e-d. Lenore played the tape, and I just sat and watched it on the television screen. I listened to a niece I'd never met comment that my birthmother had four daughters. I was totally invisible.

After that was over, the day only got more surreal. Lenore made an announcement. "I want to tell you something, I'm going to believe what my mother told me about Robert Mosier being your father. Because she would not lie to me."

Of course she wouldn't, Lenore. She just lied to you for fifty-two solid years.

It was a strange proclamation. But having been in the mental health field for so many years, I was no stranger to good old fashioned, garden-variety Denial.

Lenore's language and demeanor registered as a gauntlet being thrown down. The scene was a bit uncomfortable. Zippy was absolutely silent, watching me, then watching Lenore. Lenore was drawing a line and letting me know she was choosing Pat's version of the past over mine. Fair enough... I was no longer invested in changing anyone's mind. I had lived this outrageous tale of secrets and lies. I knew what had happened.

"We're going to have to agree to disagree," I replied. "I'd be willing to bet dinner on it." I was trying to be light-hearted and certainly was not going to take issue with her. She was entitled to her own belief.

Lenore replied, "Okay," and I headed for the door, more than ready to bring these interactions to a close.

As I exited, I said, "Lenore, you save your pennies because I really like to eat."

Prior to my birthmother passing away, I had a realization that finally landed me the court order I had wanted so desperately...the order for my original file. Why, I wondered, would the court be compelled to keep my records from me now that I had actually *met* the two people identified as my biological parents on my original birth certificate? There was no one's privacy left to "protect."

I phoned the Kay County court clerk and said, "I've met both my biological parents, and as such there are no issues of confidentiality. Do you suppose I could finally see my DHS file?" She said she would ask the judge if he would consider ordering it.

The judge came through:

*December 17, 2008; ORDER DIRECTING DEPART-MENT OF HUMAN SERVICES TO DELIVER CONFIDENTIAL RECORDS*

*NOW on this 17th day of December, 2008, the Application of Rhonda Jean Noonan for Disclosure of Confidential Records maintained in the possession of the Oklahoma Department of Human Services (DHS) as said records pertain to the adoption of Baby Girl Gafford (now Rhonda Jean Noonan) comes on for the Court's consideration. Having reviewed the pleadings herein, the Court finds:*

*There is no confidentiality to preserve and applicant desires to have a copy of any records maintained by the DHS pertaining to her adoption and any pre-adoption records pertaining to her. IT IS THEREFORE ORDERED: That the DHS of the State of Oklahoma provide to Applicant within thirty (30) days of this date any and all records maintained and preserved by DHS pertaining to Applicant's adoption or pre-adoption custody. Dated this 17th Day of December, 2008*

Surely this would give me some additional answers as to the events surrounding my actual adoption. Maybe the "hint" as to my father's identity was in there and would add even more evidence to what Polly had told me. I knew I wanted to reach out to my birthfather's family, and tell them what I had discovered. I was certain they would find the entire story, combined with Polly's statement, compelling enough to investigate a little deeper, and hopefully provide a DNA sample which would confirm or eliminate the possibility that I was of their blood.

How could I do that? How does anyone contact a family about something like this? I had no clue. So, I went online and began exploring. I contacted the Churchill Center in Chicago, and enlisted the aid of a woman named Mary Paxton. She's responsible for forwarding mail to the Churchill family. In January 2009, I wrote them a letter, and sent it to Mary.

*Dear Churchill family:*

*It is with excitement and some disbelief that I write to tell you of my recent discovery.*

*I am an adult adoptee, 52 years of age, living in a small town outside Tulsa, Oklahoma. I was adopted through the Oklahoma Department of Human Services in 1956. For approximately thirty years I have searched for my biological family, following bits and pieces of a story that was told to me as a child. My biological mother is still living outside of Oklahoma City (she is 93 years of age). We met this past year; however, she was unwilling to share my father's identity with me, or discuss the experience she had.*

*Last month, I was finally, after 22 years, able to obtain a court order to release all of the state's records to me. My search has involved interviewing the children of former state officials, scouring archives, interviewing the last living case worker involved in the adoption as well as the children of several caseworkers now deceased, and gathering information provided by a CIA employee. I had known for many years the FBI was involved in the adoption, interviewing my maternal grandparents and town businessmen. I knew my adoptive parents' phone had been tapped and that their dealings with the State Department were far from "normal" when adopting a baby. Former President Harry Truman played a role in helping to place me.*

*It is my belief that I am the daughter of Randolph Churchill. My birthmother was involved in a brief encounter with him in October of 1955 after an evening at the Tinker Air Force Base Officer's Club. I was adopted by Jim and Jeanlee Noonan of Tonkawa, Oklahoma, and was raised in a loving, healthy home. I am a licensed mental health clinician and serve as*

*Clinical Director at Shadow Mountain Behavioral Health System in Tulsa, Oklahoma, an inpatient psychiatric facility for children and teenagers.*

*I realize this comes as unexpected news...It certainly was a surprise to me. It is not my desire to create an upset in the family. I simply wanted you to know, and to introduce myself. If you would like to correspond, I would enjoy that very much.*

*With Sincerest Regards,*

*Rhonda Noonan*

*CC: Lady Mary Soames, Winston Churchill II, Honorable Celia Sandys*

Mary Paxton would inform me as each recipient confirmed their receipt of the letters.

I waited for a response. For anything—a single word.

And I waited.

And waited...

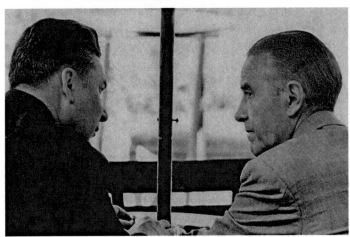

*This page, top: Pat Nail.*
*Bottom: Averell Harriman and Raymond Gary.*
*Opposite page: Randolph in uniform.*

*Opposite: Randolph with Arabella and Winston.*
*This page: A Churchill family photo.*

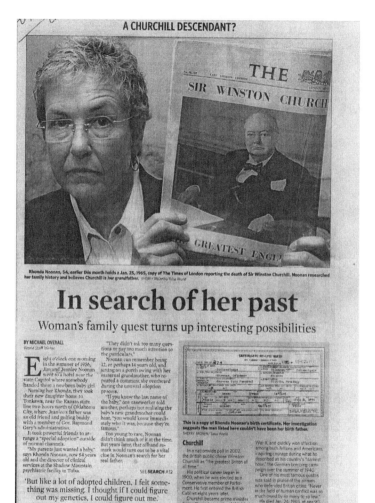

*Opposite: Randolph poses with his own book.*
*This page: The local paper,* Tulsa World,
*covers the story of my journey.*

*Opposite: Alison Larkin and me in 2009.*
*This page: My grandfather, Winston Churchill.*

"The first quality that is needed
is audacity."

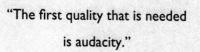

*Winston Churchill*

# "Time to dare and endure"

The month of February passed without receiving any response from the Churchills.

I pressed forward with a Freedom of Information-Privacy Act Request. On March 3, 2009, I received a letter from the Federal Bureau of Investigation regarding my request (#1127007-000). The FBI said they had received my petition, and would contact me with more information.

I decided to reach out to the Churchills again. At the beginning of March, I wrote another letter:

*Dear Churchill family,*

*My letter of January 30, came, no doubt, as a considerable surprise. As more time has gone by, and more details have come to light, I thought I would write and let you all know how things are progressing.*

*My birthmother has, finally, offered some information, and I am awaiting the arrival of the FBI file that outlines, more completely, the details of the months prior to my birth. I will be glad to provide you all with a copy so that you will understand what transpired as well.*

*I am completing the application to formalize my British citizenship and will be making a trip over to participate in the ceremony. My travels have never included Britain and it will be an adventure to explore this part of my heritage.*

*Again, I just wanted to contact you and welcome
communication. You may contact me by e-mail.*
*Sincerely,*
*Rhonda Noonan*
CC: Lady Mary Soames, Winston S. Churchill, Celia
Sandy.

A few weeks later, I received notice from the U.S. Department of Justice that my administrative appeal from the action of the FBI had been received and was assigned an appeal number: 09-1489. The letter ended, "We will notify you of the decision of your appeal as soon as we can. We regret the necessity of this delay and appreciate your continued patience."

Approximately two weeks later a letter arrived from the Bureau stating, again, that they have no record of anything involving me, my adoptive family, Randolph Churchill, or Irene Pruitt-Gafford in their archives. I contacted our state FBI office and discussed it with agents. They stated "those kinds of things" might never "have been recorded anywhere."

*Clearly*, I thought.

The Churchill Center of Chicago had a website I frequented. One day I saw mention of a polo match in Connecticut. The article announced that the guest of honor would be my half-brother, Winston Churchill. His son Randolph was to be there as well.

The instant I read it, I knew that nothing could stop me from attending that event. I immediately started checking on flights and tickets, and called my old friend Denna who agreed to come with me. My mom also agreed to go, but she didn't want to fly, so we decided to take a road trip.

My previous two letters to the Churchill family had gone unanswered, and I knew they had received them. So I drafted a letter to Winston that I could hand-deliver. I also prepared a letter for Randolph.

*June 4, 2009*
*Dear Winston:*

*A few months have passed since I last sent you a letter, telling you about my search for my biological parents and the discovery that you and I share the same father. A former supervisor for Oklahoma's Department of Human Services first confirmed my father's identity when she recalled a meeting between State of Oklahoma adoption officials, Randolph Churchill, and herself in 1956.*

*For years, the pursuit of my own personal truth and the absolute refusal to give up has propelled me forward through countless roadblocks and challenges. Indeed, the facts surrounding my birth and adoption are so intriguing that an author friend of mine has taken interest in developing a book on the subject. I believe that you, too, will find my life story fascinating.*

*I have come here to Connecticut to see both you and Randolph, and hope to meet with you to explain how this story has evolved from mysterious hints and suggestions years ago, to being here today. I am staying near the polo field at the Hyatt Regency until Monday morning, and hope you find your way clear to visit with me. The number here is, etc., or you may call me anytime on my personal cell phone.*

*Very sincerely yours,*
*Rhonda Noonan*

The polo game was on a Saturday. We arrived in Connecticut on the Thursday prior, so we had Friday to do whatever we wanted. We checked into the Hyatt Regency in Greenwich and decided to take the train to New York City. The train trip was less than an hour—straight into to Grand Central Station.

Having never been to Manhattan, we loved it. I was mesmerized, and Mom was absolutely tickled pink. Denna had been there before and really enjoyed seeing it again. We visited Times Square and the Statue of Liberty, and walked all over town. Mom could out-walk both Denna and me (and she has thirty years on both of us!).

The air of New York was electric. The people, the pulse—everything thrummed. I loved seeing my mom so enchanted with the sights and the sheer energy. We boarded the train back to Greenwich that night, and we were beat. On the way back, we looked for the polo field so that I might find it more easily the next day.

We arose to a lovely morning, showered, dressed, and turned on the television, where the news commentator was talking about D-Day. I hadn't even realized what the date was. My focus had been squarely on this polo event. But it was in fact D-Day, so they had several people talking about the invasion of Normandy, and there—staring back at me across the movable breakfast table—was my brother, Winston. His face was on the television. I just kept looking at him. My mom was in the bathroom, and I called to her to hurry and come see. "There's my brother!"

We arrived at the polo field early, where a gargantuan tent was erected to shelter a fantastic spread. The lawn was immaculate. There were designer sofas on the lawn, and champagne and cigars were freely available. It was incredibly opulent, and hot as hell.

They ushered us to the very far corner table—as far as you could get from the front. And they placed a security guard directly behind me. Was it simply my paranoia, or did they know I was coming? And did they not like it, or think I was a nut? I wondered for a moment if it was just a coincidence...but you know how I feel about that.

I replayed my behavior, my attempts to talk with them, and could not imagine why they would be worried enough about me to place a watchdog nearby, but what did I know? This was uncharted territory for me. Surely they wouldn't assume they needed protection from me. But, I told myself in an attempt to feel okay about it, they would have no way to know for sure.

Winston had not yet arrived but they had prepared his table, sequestered behind a small picket fence in the center of things. We were among the first four or five people to arrive. The staff immediately brought out all kinds of food. I looked for Mary Paxton, who was supposed to be there, and who had said she would introduce me to Winston. But she did not come to the match after all.

I heard them say early on that Winston had gotten lost on his way. Soon a short, balding young man entered the tent, and a murmur ensued. "There's Randolph." I heard someone whisper.

"Hello." I went right up to him and shook his hand. He was a short fellow, with a fair, shaven face, large eyes, and very friendly demeanor—at least initially. I introduced myself and told him I would like to talk with him before the day was over and that I had something for him, showing him the envelope with his letter in it. He said, "All right...I will get it later...I am really thirsty. I need to get something to drink and I will get with you later." I told him I didn't want to miss talking with him. He said, "Okay, then...later on." People were chatting and buzzing around congenially.

Winston arrived later and had four or five women in tow, including his wife, Luce. I knew him immediately and prayed he would talk with me. Cigar smoke wafted through the crowd, a silent auction attracted browsers, people mingled and enjoyed the day—and all in spite of the insufferable heat.

The past twenty-eight years played through my mind, with all the frustrations and challenges. Here I was, looking right at my brother and my nephew. I wondered again if they were aware that I would be there. Randolph had been very friendly. He didn't seem guarded about anything. Had they checked the guest list and seen that I had purchased tickets? Their behavior answered that question as the afternoon unfolded.

I kept waiting for an opportune moment to deliver my letter to Winston. At one point, he was standing by himself looking at items to be auctioned. I approached him.

"Winston...Winston!"

He ignored me and walked swiftly back into the swarm of people accompanying him. I returned to my seat. I was perplexed, as he was seemingly open and friendly with other guests. People were approaching him, introducing themselves and taking pictures with him.

"I know he could hear me," I told Denna.

Then Winston went directly to his table behind the picket fence, and fetched his empty plate. Right outside the gate were the tables of food, which he now approached.

I walked up to the table across from him. As soon as I got within talking distance, he turned on his heel and returned to his seat. I thought, *Gosh, if I stay here, I guess he won't eat lunch at all!* He had literally ignored me as if I were invisible.

I had called his name twice as I approached this second time. And he still didn't respond. It was clear he wasn't going to get close enough for me to give him anything. I felt certain, at that point, that he knew exactly who I was.

Winston's table was in clear view of me, and Denna reported that he watched me intently. In the meantime Randolph, who was seated with his father, was also looking my way. My brother got up to give his talk, and he talked about our grandfather's account of D-Day, and the things he had done with him as a child. Life as a Churchill...I was riveted. I loved listening to him, despite the surreal unfolding of the day. I loved being a part of all of it.

I looked at photos of my grandfather lining the tent and loved him. That's the only way I can put it. I was so proud and felt so close to this man the world sees as a hero, and I know as my grandpa. Sound extraterrestrial? You have no idea....

I got up and took a photo. I made a point of not making eye contact with Winston. Denna reported later than he sat looking at me much of the time. I wondered what he saw. What familiarity?

All at once, one of the women who had been with him came over to the table where I was, and said, "I have seen you approach Mr. Churchill with your copy of his book. Would you like him to sign it?"

I replied, "No. I would like you to introduce me to him."

She said, "Well, I can't do that but I can take your book to him." I wanted to SCREAM! I wanted to stand up and let everyone there know the truth: *I am his sister, you knucklehead!! I want to talk to my brother!* When the very sweet couple from Texas who were seated across from me at our table inquired as to why I had driven all the way to Connecticut, I wanted to say, *Because that's my brother up there!*

However, I did none of it. I handed her the book and told her about the letter. She said she would give it to him. I watched as she delivered it. Winston kept the letter and signed the book.

She brought it back to me. The flyleaf was inscribed, "Best Wishes, Winston Churchill."

After he spoke, it was time for polo but the field was too wet to sustain a match. It had been decided that the riders would instead do a demonstration of polo fundamentals for the crowd. They mounted and people rose from the tables and moved toward the field. Randolph got up and did the same, shaking hands along the way. I approached Randolph. He had been having pictures taken with the crowd.

"Randolph," I said, "can I get a picture with you?"

I kept walking toward him, but he moved steadily away. I got louder and louder until it must have been very uncomfortable for him to ignore me with people watching. He stopped for a moment and Denna quickly took a photo. He was six feet away from me and wouldn't get any closer. It would have been comical under other circumstances.

"Randolph, I have something for you," I said, displaying the letter.

He declined it with a dismissive wave of his hand as he walked off.

At that very moment I felt a shift within me. Who do these arrogant people think they are? I have been nothing but patient, open, and honest. Surely I deserve a conversation. A *word*. I'm certain that learning one might have a long-lost relative can come as a shock, but they had known of me for some time, as I had written them and explained why I believe I am Randolph's daughter. I didn't know if it was a British thing, or a wealthy-family thing, but as far as this adopted Oklahoma Churchill was concerned, it was an inconsiderate thing.

"Come on, we're leaving," I told Denna.

"Are you kidding me? We came all this way, and now we're going?" She was shocked, and looked at me with great intensity. I was just sitting there staring at the crowd of people swarming Randolph and Winston. I begin to laugh out loud. Uncontrollably.

I had decided on my exit strategy: I left the letter right there on a table—in the middle of the socialites who had been clamoring around Randolph all afternoon. It had, in giant letters, "Randolph Churchill" printed on it. No doubt those folks will beat a path to him to make sure he doesn't leave his letter. It would be such an honor for them to deliver this sealed envelope! The thought of someone opening it and reading the contents or chasing him through the tent with it was hilarious to me. Call it nerves, or frustration, or simply being at the end of my *very long* rope, I couldn't stop laughing at the cartoon playing through my head. I know Mom and Denna must have thought I'd lost my mind.

I didn't want to make a scene or embarrass anyone or make anyone uncomfortable. I was going to take the high road, and just leave. I kept telling myself that truth is on my side, and my day would come. I was certain of it.

We got in the car and left.

"But like a lot of adopted children,

I felt something was missing.

I thought if I could figure out my genetics,

I could figure out me."

———

*Rhonda Noonan*, Tulsa World,

*August 16, 2010*

# "Going on swinging bravely"

A friend who worked with me at the psychiatric hospital had a meeting with a man named Steve Turnbo to talk about a marketing plan for the entire hospital. During their meeting, Steve told my friend about a project of his, and some ideas he was implementing related to promoting a book. My friend said: "If you want a story worth promoting, talk to my friend Rhonda, who just found out she's Winston Churchill's granddaughter."

Steve Turnbo was interested. He worked at a Tulsa public relations firm and was a well-respected leader in the community.

My friend handed me Steve's card, and told me to contact him; that he wanted to talk to me.

I called Steve and told him the highlights of the entire story, and explained that I had piles of documentation to back it all up.

As we talked, the idea of a newspaper article was explored. It would be distributed via the Associated Press. I said, "I'm game."

I had tried in every way I knew possible to open communication with my family. I had sent three letters, I had approached them face to face, and they totally ignored me. I was ready to go public with my story, but there was no point in drawing a lot of attention to my story if it didn't translate to adoption-issue awareness that might one day translate into legislative change in adoptive rights and services.

I knew it was my calling to work as an advocate for adult adoptees—to change the laws, to push the system, to fight for their civil rights. I knew, as every adoptee in America knows, that we are second-class citizens. We don't even have authentic birth certificates. I knew that what we were fighting for was fundamentally about human rights. I wanted to use my own life story to create a conversation which would lead to individuals learning their truth.

I did not believe the Churchills would ever step up and have any kind of relationship with me. I was left with nothing but my story.

I shared with Steve that I wanted to tell the complete journey in a book, but had no idea how to proceed. So before we approached any newspapers, he helped by making calls to some authors. One was simply too busy to deal with it. Another was seemingly intimidated by the scope of it and what the Churchill family might think.

I was frustrated more and more by seemingly infinite dead ends. I talked to a local publishing company that was more than willing and excited about the story, but they wanted the complete rights to it.

Steve was incredibly kind and very helpful. He suggested that *The Tulsa World* might be interested in telling the story. They were, and they ran an article about me on the front page of the "Living" section. That was picked up by the AP, and made it around the world in an instant. It was soon being commented on in Churchill chat groups.

A few days after the piece was published, I got an email from a fellow in Southern Illinois. He was a retired grandfather—a computer guy. He had read my story, and wrote to ask, "Do you mind if I try to help you?"

"Not at all, I'd love it." I said. I was thrilled that he would offer. A few days later I got another email from him with a link to Michael Sands' website. Michael is a public relations professional, working out of Beverly Hills.

"Are you okay with me giving him your phone number?" the man asked.

"Sure, give it to him." I wanted any lead I could get.

Michael Sands called me. He was interested in my story because he had been friends with my half-sister, Arabella Churchill. She had once hired him to produce an online video broadcast of her facelift. Before the surgery occurred, she cancelled due to poor health. Michael had remained friendly with her and exchanged emails and cards. He also knew her husband, Haggis McLeod. Michael said, "Let me talk to Haggis, and see if I can maybe help you get some DNA from the Churchill family."

Michael was hoping that the Churchills would do the right thing. I told Michael they had obfuscated and stonewalled and eschewed any type of contact. I shared that I knew they had received my letters, because they had acknowledged as much to Mary Paxton. Michael said he would call Mary himself and ask to speak with Randolph about the issue. Mary agreed to contact Randolph and let him know that Michael wished to talk with him.

In the meantime, my brother Winston died of cancer. And Polly died of old age. Time was marching on. My sister Arabella had died in 2007. That was a hard one for me. It was hard for me to think that I could not meet her; that it had taken me so long to get to the truth. That I couldn't find this out fast enough. That I had run out of time.

Randolph Churchill responded that "he needed time to think about" Michael's request to talk. And then he never responded. Meanwhile, Michael sent Haggis an email asking for help securing some DNA.

Haggis told Michael, "Tell Rhonda she can email me." Michael gave me the address, and I was *thrilled*! I immediately composed an email:

*Greetings Haggis!*

*Rhonda Noonan here. I am so grateful to be making your acquaintance via email. Michael tells me you are very busy, doing some incredible work... so thank you for allowing me to say hello. A good friend of mine is currently in India, working for the Lakshya Trust, doing similar work on the front lines. Incredibly important, and, at times overwhelming.*

*As I'm sure you know, my search for my biological family spans more than 28 years. Of all my biological siblings, Arabella was the one person I felt I probably had the most in common with. Everything I have read and heard about her suggests she was an extraordinary human being. The fact that she passed so young saddens me deeply and I thank you, again, for allowing me to express this to you. It's one of those dynamics that, if you're not adopted and missing your "roots," probably doesn't make a lot of sense. It is what it is.*

*Like Arabella, much of my time, energy, and focus in my life is children. I run the clinical aspects of a psychiatric hospital for kids 4-18 years of age, and am a specialist in adoption/attachment issues. Hopefully, in the near future, Michael and I can fly over to meet you and your daughter Jessica.*

*All the best,*

*Rhonda*

I thought the message was very warm and filled with gratitude, conveying my appreciation for his willingness to communicate. But I never heard a word from him—not a return email, nothing. Michael sent an email to see if Haggis was going to help us, and Haggis responded with a doozy. He seemed to not understand why I would want to talk to him and took exception to Michael referring to him as a friend in correspondence with Randolph. Haggis wanted no more contact regarding me and expressed his desire to be "clear."

Michael's feelings were really hurt by the tone of Haggis' response. "We weren't as close as I was with Arabella, but I felt like Haggis and I were friends," he said.

I fired back my own response to Haggis:

*December 2, 2010*
*Dear Haggis,*

*If you do not understand why I would treasure meeting you, then you do not understand any of this at all. You were my sister's husband; a sister I will never know except through those who knew her. Your daughter is my niece. Randolph is my nephew, etc., etc., etc. My family. It is that simple. I don't have some big hidden agenda. I am very much a "what you see is what you get" kind of person. I tend to not mince my words and tell the truth. Period. Finding out where I came from has helped me, in many ways, understand myself—why I am the way I am, why I perceive the world the way I do, why I look the way I look...all of the things that people, who can be a part of their families, take for granted and don't even think twice about. I have been able to gain insight because I can read about my dad and read about my grandpa due to their fame. And I have read a lot about them both; every book about my dad and a lot about my grandpa. I suppose, under these circumstances, that is one good thing about them being famous. If no one cares to meet me, at least I can know something about them. Unfortunately, there isn't a lot out there about Arabella. That's where Michael came in. He knew her. It was an opportunity for me to talk with someone who had actually talked to my sister. That was HUGE for me.*

*As for Michael and Randolph, etc., Michael is just trying to help me. Neither of us wants to create problems for you. You have my word I will not contact you again. No worries. Actually, I don't know what this has to do with Randolph. I traveled to Connecticut to offer my brother and Randolph a chance to meet me and talk with me. I shook Randolph's hand and tried to give him a letter I wrote to explain some of what happened that led to my discovery of my history. Neither of them took the opportunity to talk and acted like I was infected with a horrid, contagious disease they would certainly catch if they got too close. It was really quite ridiculous. I guess I don't understand what the big concern is. I have been incredibly patient and truthful about everything while I have been ignored and treated as though I am some kind of stalker or lunatic. It is what it is. As my grandfather said, "The truth is incontrovertible. Panic may resent it, ignorance may deride it, malice may distort it, but there it is." I am appalled that no one in the family seems to value the truth; indeed they are not even interested in it.*

*I knew, early on, that I had a grandfather who wanted me and had been enraged over how the situation with me was handled. I knew my mother didn't want to see me and my father didn't care about me, but my grandfather did. For 28 years, I turned over every clue, every hint, and every lead to find the truth. As you might imagine, discovering that the grandfather I had so wanted to find all that time was Winston Churchill, was a bit hard to wrap around. Sometimes I still feel numb about it all; as though I am living in some sort of parallel universe and none of this has really happened. But it has. I actually know quite a*

*bit about how it all came down. I wanted to discuss
that with my brother before the book came out so that
he could comment and there could be some collabora-
tion, but it wasn't to be. So, the truth will be told—as
it was told to me and I experienced it, from the beginning, all through the years to this day. I guess my
family can read it along with everyone else.*

*I hope I've made myself clear.*

*Best to You,*
*Rhonda Gafford Schultz*
*Mosier Noonan*
*CHURCHILL*

No sooner had I hit "send" on that email to Haggis when
Michael texted me. The message was, "Here you go…" and
the attachment was a forwarded text he had just received: the
long-awaited request from the *Independent,* a well-respected
London newspaper, for an interview. One door had slammed
shut, and I quietly thanked God for opening another.

Michael called and explained how this had come to pass.
"The L.A. correspondent for the *Independent* called me for a
quote about another client. But I wanted him to talk to you.
His name is Guy Adams."

Guy phoned me and we talked for at least an hour. He
wrote the story, and the *Independent* published it. The thing
that really startled me was just how much interest there was
in it. It remained their fourth most-read story for a whole
weekend. Many people from the U.K. contacted me. And their
comments were more encouraging than disparaging.

A couple of days after the story ran, I was contacted by
Fox News in Tulsa. They wanted to do a segment on me and
came to the house to film it. It was a fairly lengthy interview
that in my opinion went well. I was beginning to get my story
out, but I knew I had to tell the *whole* story…in a book.

Leroy Bridges was a historian and a personal friend of Gerdy Gary, Governor Gary's son. Leroy was, I was told, a political historian who had worked with most of the great world leaders of the twentieth century. He was currently at the University of Oklahoma. Gerdy had suggested, during Linda's call to him, that I visit with Leroy, as he thought the scholar might have some thoughts on how to help me. Gerdy commented that, if anyone would know anything about a situation with a baby and Randolph Churchill, it would be Leroy.

I agreed that would be wonderful and he had Leroy call me. He asked if I would have lunch with him at the Oklahoma University Faculty Lounge. I met him two weeks later and I told him an abbreviated version of my story. Later, as we chatted at the table, I asked, "When I told you my story, what did you think of it? What did you think of me?...And I want the truth."

Without hesitation, he replied, "I thought, *This is Winston Churchill's granddaughter.*"

Leroy had access to a lot of the state's historical archives. He wanted to do some checking to make sure there wasn't information available that no one had thought to access. He also solicited the help of a friend, Bob McDonald, who had been an attorney for the state for years and was quite a history buff and a fan of Winston Churchill. He was interested in the story of my search and wanted to help. They laid out a plan to check some historical archives at the capitol building.

This was all very encouraging, but I was doubtful anything would be uncovered that would add support to my discovery. It was nice, however, to feel enthusiasm and validation.

As we neared the end of our lunch, Leroy asked if he could have a picture taken with me. I said of course, though I wondered why he wanted it. We stood in front of the OU seal while a photographer snapped away.

Returning to the table, LeRoy stopped to have a word with a friend he'd spotted. I told him I would wait at the table.

As I sat, the maitre d' came over and said, "Ms. Churchill, it's been wonderful having you here today. Is there anything else I can do for you?"

I looked at him with absolute shock. I was stunned. "No, thank you. You are very kind."

He continued, "It is an honor to have you with us today."

*Wow,* I thought. *Someone using my real name.*

After years of what can only be described as low-grade frustration and pushing on against adversity, that small interaction, with a kind stranger, soothed my soul. It was affirming and encouraging. It alleviated my depression and frustration and propelled me forward. My internal quest for knowledge had met my truth.

"It is enough to simply need to know who you are. And every once in a while you find somebody really interesting on the other end."

———

*Rhonda Noonan*
*(at a legislative committee hearing on an adoptee's rights to open records)*
The Oklahoman, *October 12, 2011*

# "The empires of the future"

L ast November I was having lunch with Samantha Franklin, the Oklahoma representative for the American Adoption Congress. We were sitting at lunch talking about how the general public knows so little about what it's like as an adult to be treated like a child. (The very phrase "adopted child" is often used to describe grownups. When did you last hear someone say "adopted adult"?) And, while some states do have open records, Oklahoma's thinking is archaic. We knew we needed to change the way people think.

We decided to design and conduct our own workshop. I asked Samantha if she knew people who would be able to discuss adoption in a way that was palatable in a state with these policies. She said she had been to a workshop featuring a performance by a British woman who had been born in the United States. The woman's name was Alison Larkin.

I was captivated by the idea of someone with a history that was basically my story in reverse. I went back to the office and approached our CEO about authorizing sponsorship for the workshop. Meanwhile I got online to check into booking Alison Larkin for our event. I found a link on her website and contacted her agent.

She was not only brilliant, literate, and witty, she was also an incredibly talented actress who had written and performed her own one-woman show. We wanted to book her for a performance of some of the material from that show, and maybe to deliver a keynote address at our workshop during the conference.

I was thrilled when Alison phoned me back. I missed the call, but she left me a message basically saying that her agent had given her some information about our event, and because of the subject matter she would be happy to discuss it.

I called her back and we chatted for a while. We discussed possible dates and professional expectations for the conference. She asked, "Are you an adoptee?"

"Yes," I said.

"Have you ever searched for your bio parents?"

"Yes I have."

"Was it a meaningful experience for you?"

"As a matter of fact, it was."

"Did you find your biological family?"

"Yes…in fact I discovered that my father is Randolph Churchill."

There was a long pause at the other end.

"You *are* kidding me, right?" she asked.

"No, ma'am, I'm quite serious," I assured her.

"Randolph Churchill, the son of Sir Winston Churchill?"

"One and the same."

"I'm going tell my agent that I'm dealing with you directly. You have my phone number and my email address, let's talk more and see what we can do. It will be an honor to work with Sir Winston's granddaughter."

Over the next two months we continued talking, sharing notes and ideas about the workshop. We decided a fun workshop title would be "Lunch with the English Americans." We would each share our experiences with search and reunion.

Alison was perfect for this event, because she had written a book called *The English American*, based on her life experiences, which told the story of her search for her American birthparents after having been raised abroad.

The morning was a fantastic success, and while the participants were eating lunch Alison and I talked about our lives, and how much it had meant to us to search for our ancestors and unearth our histories.

The performance that evening was nothing short of magical. Alison performed "An Evening with Alison Larkin" at the theater facility at Union High School. She was marvelous; the audience was rapt, and exploded into a standing ovation when she finished.

The evening's schedule also included an award presentation. We honored the legendary searcher, and my dear friend, Linda Colvard with a lifetime achievement award on behalf of all the adoptees she had helped. We invited as many of them to attend as possible. The inscription on her award read:

*PRESENTED TO LINDA COLVARD*
*For your countless hours of selfless giving*
*and tenacious pursuit of truth,*
*with heartfelt gratitude and love,*
*Your adoptees*

Alison presented her the beautiful glass sculpture. Linda was totally surprised and delighted. The entire day—both the workshop and the conference—were smashing successes. I felt that, finally, adult adoptees had a voice—a forum—of their own.

Our workshops had included topics such as how to search, resolving early trauma, and addressing grief and loss.There was a suicide prevention workshop, and a section on networking to improve resources and support. It was wonderful.

That day I realized, at a newer and deeper level, that a huge part of my mission in this world is indeed to assist adult adoptees.

Between Alison's show and Linda's award, it was about as perfect as a day could be for me. I headed home with my head in the clouds. I walked into the house, and the words of Alison Larkin resonated within me: "You have a right to tell your story."

The statement echoed in my heart with a new simplicity and profundity. Of course. You can steal everything else from me—my history, my name, my identity, my ancestry—but you cannot steal my story. It is mine and I have a right to tell it...for all the adoptees who have searched and hoped and dreamed. For all of the decision-makers who do not understand the importance of knowing the *truth*....

I sat down at my laptop, and as I started typing the voice of one of the the greatest characters in English literature thundered in my head: "Chapter One...To begin my life with the beginning of my life, I record that I was born (as I have been informed and believe) on a Friday, at twelve o'clock at night. It was remarked that the clock began to strike, and I began to cry, simultaneously...."

"I see you getting a letter from a perfect stranger with a lot of information. It will be the truth and you can check it out. You will sign papers and see a lawyer. You will travel and see your family. Somebody is going to try to tell the truth. They put a new guy in there and he's going to try to figure it out. You will be a hero to many people and I will be with you until this all comes to pass...."

———

*Lillie, 2008*

CPSIA information can be obtained at www.ICGtesting.com
Printed in the USA
BVOW071205040613

322406BV00001B/13/P